Attachment in the classroom

The links between children's early experience, emotional well-being and performance in school

Heather Geddes

Worth Publishing

www.worthpublishing.com

First published 2006 by Worth Publishing Ltd
9 Charlotte Road, London SW13 9QJ
www.worthpublishing.com

Reprinted 2007, 2008

Printed and bound in Great Britain by Biddles, King's Lynn, UK

British Library Cataloguing in Publication Data
A catalogue record for this book is available from the British Library

ISBN 978-1-903269-08-4

Cover and text design by Anna Murphy
Cover image by Poppy Norrish

To Samantha and Ben

Acknowledgements

The content of this book is supported by innumerable glimpses into work with children, families and teachers over many years and in different settings. It is this which underpins my responses and practice and continues to drive my interest. I would like to acknowledge my gratitude and respect to all those whose work and experience is reflected here. I wish to thank the participants of the 'Attachment in the Classroom' workshop in London earlier this year, who gave their time to reflecting on the interventions discussed here and generously donated ideas of their own: Sue Binham, Myra Bird, Barbara Earl, Louise Holland, Gloria Holland, Jane Huckstep, Hilda Mendoza, Veronica Read, Jane Riordan, Ruth Robertson, Sue Rowe, Lynne Rowson, Tess Tatham, Vaughan Titheridge, Jane Waring, Clair Waterhouse and Trisha Waters.

I have also gained enormously from colleagues with whom I have worked closely over the years at the Caspari Foundation, London, where there is continuous discussion, reflection and teaching about issues in educational therapy practice.

I would particularly like to thank Paul McKeever whose originality and intelligence first encouraged the quest to understand the learning difficulties of the challenging young people we worked with: Professor Ron Best who supported me through the complex challenges of research: Juliet Hopkins and Mary-Sue Moore who have supported the development of my understanding of Attachment issues: Elaine Arnold who has inspired my interest in the challenges and difficulties of Afro-Caribbean children today and the friends, relatives and colleagues who have sustained me during the experience of writing this book.

Dr Heather Geddes Teachers' Cert, MA, PhD, UKCP Reg., is an educational therapist and has worked as a teacher and Educational Therapist in a variety of settings in education, Child Guidance and Child and Adolescent Mental Health Services. She also works privately as a therapist, supervisor and trainer and contributes to the M.A. Training in Educational Therapy at the Caspari Foundation.

Her interest in the pupil's experience of learning began in her own primary school where she witnessed the humiliation of those children who could not learn. Later, when a teacher in a large girls' comprehensive school, she was reminded of this and found herself more interested in the difficulties of pupils who could not learn and the challenges that their behaviour presented. This led to work in a Social Services led Intermediate Treatment Centre with youngsters at risk where she was able to focus on individual difficulties which interfered with the capacity to think and to learn. Curiosity about failure in learning led to training as an Educational Therapist. This enabled her to engage in the emotional and social experiences which can impede learning, hence her move into Child Guidance Units and a focus on intervention in early years.

Her research thesis identified links between early Attachment experience and particular patterns of response in the classroom to the teacher and to the learning task.

Her particular field of interest is the effects of emotional experience on children's capacities to learn, and the implications of Attachment patterns in particular.

Contents

(continues ...)

Contents (continued)

Chapter 1

Making a Difference
Attachment Theory and the pupils who trouble us

Introduction

Brian, aged nine, sat in the corner of the classroom at a table on his own, looking away from the class. He had been put there to stop him bothering other children and disrupting the lesson with his denigrating remarks to others, and his interruption of the teacher. He had the attention of a Learning Support Assistant but did not let her help him. Instead he stabbed at the paper with his pencil as if he were attacking the task rather than trying to think about it. As usual, at break he was in trouble for an unprovoked attack on another boy. He denied doing it and said the boy provoked him. His mother thought his behaviour must be the fault of the school and the way the staff handled him.

Teachers are only too familiar with pupils with social and emotional difficulties and with pupils with behavioural difficulties in particular. The implications of challenging pupil behaviour for teachers and for other pupils is a serious issue. At the mild end of the continuum, are the pupils who take time to adjust to classroom routines and school rules. In time, and with consistent boundaries, practices and rituals, these pupils can learn to conform to expectations and become focused on learning. Another group of pupils responds to more specialised intervention, such as focused in-class intervention or small withdrawal groups. However, a significant number of pupils fail to respond to best practice. At the more extreme end of the continuum, pupils can disrupt the class and de-skill the teacher. Very often, exclusion seems the only option.

This is not a new problem. There is a long history of concern about pupils with emotional, social and behavioural difficulties who underachieve in school. The negative implications of this are extensive; for the pupil for whom underachieving can lead to withdrawal, disaffection and social exclusion: for the teacher, who can feel de-skilled, disheartened and stressed: for families, who can feel persecuted and helpless over complaints about their children: for the measurement of school performance, and for society in general, in terms of diminished mental health of young people and the cost to society.

Behaviour is usually the factor which leads concerns about pupils. History reflects a gradual shift from interventions outside school to a policy of 'inclusion', which does not always reflect the needs of the pupil nor the professional and personal readiness of the teachers and education staff.

Over some years, working in a range of education and health settings, it has been my experience that teachers are perfectly able to teach almost all pupils. With a greater insight into the meaning and implications of pupils' emotional and social difficulties, the teacher's capacity to respond to the pupil changes, and the pupil can become more accessible to teaching. For the pupil, school can be changed from a negative experience to one in which he or she can achieve, and in which his or her self-esteem can be enhanced. These experiences increase resilience and hopefulness.

The approach described here is informed by a psychoanalytic perspective and emerges from the standpoint of educational therapy practice. It seeks to contribute to a better understanding of pupil behaviour. Teachers are not expected to become therapists! but teachers can work therapeutically with greater insight into and understanding of pupils' difficulties and experiences. This is not so much a book about 'what to do' but rather about 'how to think about the problem', to achieve a more hopeful outcome – changing from being reactive to being reflective, so that reflection leads practice.

- This book seeks to explore the **social and emotional experiences** which drive pupil behaviour in a way that can contribute to the teacher's understanding of the pupil, and so contribute to their responses, both personally and educationally.

- The basic premise is that **behaviour has meaning** – whether it is provocative and reactive, or withdrawn and silent. Understanding the communication implicit in behaviour can protect the teacher from being adversely affected by pupil's feelings and defensive patterns, and can thus enhance practice and pupil achievement.

- Over the last forty years, **Attachment Theory** has become a major developmental paradigm for understanding human social and emotional development. John Bowlby is regarded as the 'father' of Attachment Theory. From his original premise of the implications of 'maternal deprivation', to research techniques which can identify patterns of relationships between infants and primary carers, a greater understanding of the influence of very early relationships has emerged which is linked directly to expectations and responses in school. These findings, supported by comments from clinical work with children, can provide useful insight into daily classroom experience. Attachment Theory is also the basis for proposing a teacher support framework aimed at substantially changing the institutional response to challenging behaviour and its implications for teachers.

● **Attachment research** is described, identifying patterns of pupil behaviour which teachers notice in the classroom but can experience as baffling or overwhelming. These patterns are explored in terms of the implications for teaching and learning.

● **The Learning Triangle** is introduced. This reflects the relationships between the pupil, the teacher and the task, and provides a focus for the application of Attachment Theory and research.

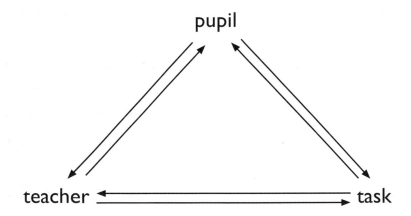

Fig. 1 The Learning Triangle

● The understanding derived from this approach is linked to proposals for **interventions** relevant to educational practice with pupils and to teacher support.

Throughout the book, examples from practice will be used to illustrate the text and to relate the contents to teachers' experiences.

The general context of teaching and learning

There has always been a problem

The development of understanding the 'problem pupil' has a long history. The response to challenging behaviour in school reflects the struggle which has gone on in education over the years to find a way of thinking about these 'hard-to-teach' pupils.

Cohen & Cohen (1986) report concerns from many years ago which are still familiar today. In 1925, teachers in one school district in New York found undesirable behaviour in over fifty percent of the pupils. In 1934, it was reported that forty-six percent of pupils in London Elementary Schools demonstrated 'behavioural deviancy'. In 1938, similar numbers of problem children were identified, but it was pointed out that there was a tendency for teachers to focus on pupils who defy teacher authority or refuse to work or co-operate, and to overlook the shy, timid or unsociable children who did not disrupt order. This work begins to point to the difficult issue of who perceives the situation as a problem and how is it defined (Cohen & Cohen p.223).

Over the years, the response to these early concerns has resulted in increased provision for 'maladjusted' pupils: Child Guidance units blossomed, places in children's homes, specialist boarding and day schools increased and the reaction to the challenge of difficult behaviour was reflected in rising exclusion rates (Garner 1993, Parsons et al. 1994). Subsequently, policies of inclusion and shrinking resources have fuelled a drive to respond more effectively to challenging behaviour within mainstream schools.

How is behaviour defined?

An extensive study was carried out in Newcastle and Gateshead schools (Kolvin et al 1981). The aim was to identify children with difficulties and to compare different ways of helping children to overcome these difficulties. The team reported that: 'in different parts of the U.K. between seven and twenty-five percent of school children are handicapped by frank psychiatric problems' (p.4). They made the distinction between *neurotic disorder* and *conduct disorder*.

Neurotic disorder was defined as one in which there is an abnormality of emotions but no loss of sense of reality (i.e. an absence of psychosis). This would include disproportionate anxiety and feelings of depressions, obsessions, compulsions, phobias, hypochondrias. This could be summarised as distress within the self.

On the other hand, a *conduct disorder* was defined as one that causes disapproval and distress in others. It was predicted that in general, the outlook for the conduct disordered child is poor and that this behaviour can precede life-long behaviour and personality disorders. In addition, conduct disorders may be associated with deviance in subsequent generations (Robins, West & Herjanic 1975).

Further investigation confirmed that socio-economic background, gender and behaviour are linked to educational under-achievement. So too is a relatively high incidence of psychiatric disorders, and the research concluded that 'probably at least one child in twenty has a significant psychiatric disorder' (Rutter et al 1979, p.178). This figure is reflected in the publication *Young Minds* (1996) concerning the mental health of schoolchildren and set out in *Promoting Children's Mental Health within Early Years and School Settings* (DfES 2001).

Who has the problem?

In a study of six thousand children in Buckingham schools (Shepherd et al. 1971) behaviour issues as well as low social class and gender were clearly identified as factors connected to poor attainment. Boys were more likely to show 'difficulties' at home and were more likely to be described as aggressive (temper tantrums, fighting, disobedience and committing destructive acts), more restless and more irritable. Girls, however, were more overtly anxious, more likely to have eating difficulties and to engage in oral activity (nail biting and finger sucking). The general conclusion from this early research was that boys in general, and boys from low socio-economic groups in particular, are at higher risk at the primary school age in terms of their emotional and social adjustment. This continues to reverberate more than thirty years later with current experience, where naughty boys are more readily identified, and quiet girls are more often overlooked.

This identification of boys as being at greater risk than girls was commented on by Moore (Caspari Foundation Lecture, May 1997) when she described premature boy babies demonstrating a greater vulnerability to stressful factors in the environment. This may predispose boys to being more reactive to stressful experience in later life. This possible constitutional factor suggests that boys may be more 'at risk' than girls and also implies that factors in the environment can contribute to the level of risk.

Ethnic over-representation

In more recent years, figures relating to exclusions have raised issues about the achievement of ethnic minority groups in education. Black, mixed race and African-Caribbean children in particular are over represented in off-site education units, in Local Authority Care and in prison. Exclusion from institution and family appears to be an aspect of response to this particular group. Boys in particular under-achieve in school especially at secondary age, and are thus prone to disaffection and social exclusion. This is a complex and sensitive social issue.

(There is further discussion of this phenomenon later in Chapter 5 linked to migration history and intergenerational acting out of separations and losses, and a reference to the role of fathers in Chapter 4).

Research findings and experience indicate that vulnerability factors associated with problem behaviour are:

- low socio-economic status
- conduct disorder
- being a boy,

and it may be added

- being a boy of black and/or Afro-Caribbean ethnicity

The neurotic disordered child and girls are more likely to remain invisible in the classroom. Children who are failing educationally are likely to be in either of these categories but the response to pupils with emotional and social difficulties in the classroom is likely to be driven by;

- the teacher response to conduct disordered boys.

The quiet girls

I walk along a school corridor, passing a pair of proud children from the Early Years unit carrying the register pouch between them as if it is the crown jewels. They smile widely as I comment on the good job they are doing. Then Sarah appears, also walking towards the office. Her face is pale and her mouth downcast. She look preoccupied and very sad. I smile and ask how is she. She looks hard at me and walks on. Later I see her with her friends, smiling in the chattering group, but I recall the misery that she seemed to exude when she was alone. No matter how hard we try to prioritise girls, there always seems to be more pressing concerns about naughty boys.

Outside inner city schools, I have observed young mums gather at the gates to collect their children. There are many single parents struggling with the challenges of bringing up several children, often with absent partners. I am aware of the problems in many families: domestic violence, abuse, teenage pregnancies and often an absence of ambition or involvement in the world outside the family and the estate.

I wonder again why we don't prioritise vulnerable young girls who may one day be the mothers of troubled boys.

There is clearly a gender issue whereby boys and girls can display their distress in very different ways, with implications for resources. In particular, I wonder about why so many families seem unable to access the opportunites available in society, why there remains a large pool of families who remain in relative poverty. According to the Financial Times report on statistical monitoring (April 24th 2005) thirty percent of Britain's children live in poverty, and half of these live in single parent families.

It is likely that many factors contribute to this, including early social and emotional experience. However, the focus of this book is behavioural challenges in school and so is most likely to represent the overall experience of boys rather than girls. In terms of interventions and resources, it may be necessary to consider positively discriminating in favour of quiet but troubled girls in order to help break cycles of disadvantage and social exclusion. In the following chapters, access to opportunity is linked to accessing learning using the framework of Attachment Theory.

What affects behaviour in school?

There remain vast areas of ignorance concerning the nature of the association between difficulties in learning and behavioural disturbance. Laslett (1977) comments, 'it is important to recognise multiple causation of maladjustment … their environment has contributed something to their condition' (p.3) and he goes on to quote from Maslow (1959): 'whatever physical or genetic causes contribute to maladjustment, it is usually the result of the absence of the fundamental support systems which are essential for the satisfactory emotional development of a child, or a breakdown of this support system' (Laslett 1977, p.3). This is reflected in the position taken in this book, in which Attachment experience is highlighted as a considerable influence on behaviour and performance in school. However, the context of learning should not be ignored and in this sense, both pupils and teachers contribute to the overall experience of learning for all the pupils in a class or school.

What does the teacher bring to the classroom?

Teacher perception of and response to pupil behaviour are at the heart of the discussion about emotional and behavioural difficulties. At a personal and professional level, teachers are affected by the challenges of pupils with emotional and behavioural difficulties. Pratt (1978) identified troubling behaviour at the top of the Stress Inventory of ten factors that teachers recognised in the classroom. Atkinson (1989) commented that disruptive behaviour has a devastating impact upon teachers that can lead to considerable stress, anxiety and absenteeism within a group of mature, competent, professional people. He goes on to recommend that 'teachers analyse themselves as individuals when meeting disruptive behaviour' and are sensitive to their own vulnerabilities and pre-occupations (p.87).

Mongon & Hart (1989) comment that 'teacher-pupil relationships are a complex affair' (p.81) and a key dimension in the experience of schooling. The quality of the relationship has implications for the teacher both emotionally and professionally, and for the pupil in terms of outcome and achievement. In Lubbe's (1986) terms, the teacher's perception of the pupil shapes and mediates the contact between them and profoundly affects the teacher's efforts to engage and motivate the pupil. It is important, therefore, that more is known about this area of interaction which is not sufficiently explored by large scale investigations. (The teacher's experience and needs are explored further in Chapter 8).

It is possible to think about the relationship between the teacher and pupil as an interaction with affect (emotional implications) and meaning. In this respect, the significance of the teacher's role is examined and discussed by Salzberger-Wittenberg, et al (1983) who described the teacher role as 'suffused with meaning' for the pupil and for the teacher. Both bring to the learning situation experiences from the past and expectations that are both helpful and destructive, derived from a history of experiences and relationships of which neither may be fully consciously aware.

Hargreaves et al. (1975) report a study by Jordan (1974) identifying two groups of teachers expressing two differing orientations – the *Deviance Provocative* and the *Deviance Insulative*. These labels refer to the response the teachers evoked in pupils, and these two major patterns of teacher response can be thought of as a continuum along which all teachers can identify their own practice.

The *Deviance Provocative* teacher was one who had a preponderance of negative attitudes towards children, was attracted towards confrontation and used humiliation as a form of control. Such behaviour contributed to feelings of rejection, failure and poor self-image that already existed for many pupils. This in turn could lead to alienation, rejection of the values of the school and disaffection. Hargreaves et al. (1985) observed that negative peer groups grew powerful in such circumstances, and disaffection and underachievement were a possible outcome.

On the other hand, the *Deviance Insulative* teacher was firm and consistent but generally liked and respected pupils and avoided public humiliation. Pupil reactions to the Deviance Insulative teacher were to feel valued, esteemed and supported with clear implications for learning.

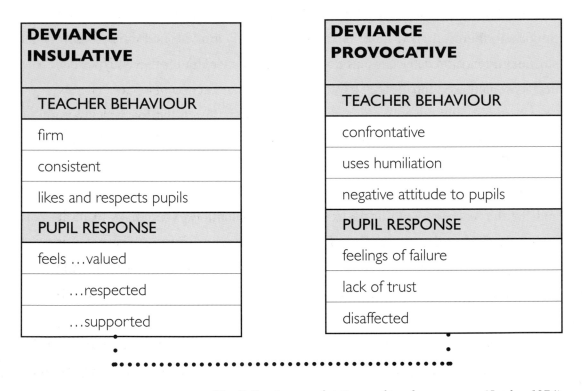

DEVIANCE INSULATIVE	DEVIANCE PROVOCATIVE
TEACHER BEHAVIOUR	**TEACHER BEHAVIOUR**
firm	confrontative
consistent	uses humiliation
likes and respects pupils	negative attitude to pupils
PUPIL RESPONSE	**PUPIL RESPONSE**
feels ...valued	feelings of failure
...respected	lack of trust
...supported	disaffected

Fig. 2 Continuum of patterns of teacher response (Jordan 1974)

This broad continuum of response to pupils, along which teachers may be able to recognise their own practice, indicates that teachers can contribute significantly to the behavioural responses of pupils and so influence the levels of possible achievement. This further reflects the need to consider the circumstances in which childrens' difficulties occur in school (the eco-systemic approach – Cooper & Upton 1991), informed by a deeper understanding of the teacher/pupil relationship.

What does the pupil bring?

Infants entering school will already have encountered experiences that will profoundly affect their relationships in school and their disposition towards learning. Dowling & Osborne (1985) describe such experiences:

> Children will have an understanding of relationships based on parents and siblings, friends and extended family. Via these they will have experienced rivalry for parental affection, sharing and ownership. They will have developed strategies for achieving satisfaction of personal needs. Children will have experiences of achievement and failure, and defences for surviving stressful situations. (p.141)

They go on to say;

> Children will already have experience of acceptable and non-acceptable behaviour and have developed a sense of morality. The more compatible the values and attitudes are between home and school, the easier a child will find the transition to school. (ibid)

Caspari (1976) comments that children soon develop behaviour that can be successful in achieving the desired attention and this can often be seen as 'bad' behaviour. As indicated previously, this then highlights the role of the teacher's reactions in perception and response to behaviour.

Emotional difficulties can result from many different experiences. Kolvin et al. (1981) point out that children will have experienced 'social hazards' such as mental ill-health in the family. In their investigation of different methods of treatment of maladjustment, they comment on 'modern society's high incidence of psychological problems' (p.3) and that the 'prevalence of disturbed children is high'. In the Sheffield study, Galloway (1982a) found high rates of psychiatric disorders, mainly depression, in parents of persistent absentees from school, and that persistent absentees came from multiply disadvantaged families (1982b). Such pre-disposing factors have been clearly identified.

PREDISPOSING FACTORS ASSOCIATED WITH CHALLENGING BEHAVIOUR
• Overt parental conflict
• Family breakdown
• Inconsistent discipline
• Hostile and rejecting relationships
• Abuse – physical, sexual or emotional
• Parental criminality, substance misuse or personality disorder
• Mental illness in the family
• Death and loss

However, it is important to consider how such experiences may affect children's behaviour and some children more than others. The framework of Attachment Theory links some of the predisposing factors listed above so that a more holistic view of pupil difficulties becomes evident.

In 1950 the Underwood Committee was appointed, 'To enquire into … the medical, educational and social problems relating to maladjusted children, with reference to their treatment within the education system'. Their report made direct references to the links between social and emotional experience and behaviour.

'Its worst effects are seen in mental hospitals, divorce courts, and prisons, since the close connection of maladjusted with disharmony in the home, delinquency and, above all, mental illness cannot be doubted' (para 15)

They went on the say that:

The part that the education service has to play in the prevention, discovery and treatment of maladjustment is of great importance.

(para 17) (Underwood Committee Report 1955)

In 1992 Benathon commented

It also needs to be widely recognised that the problems of disturbed and disruptive children inadequately helped rapidly become the problems of society. … Many mildly disturbed young people who are excluded from school could, with adequate support be helped through their difficulties. Instead they are left rejected and turn in despair to the only social groups that will give them self esteem. … They are the end result of a system which has failed to protect properly, to nurture, to educate (p. 48-9)

Both these comments, spanning several decades, highlight the importance of the educational years for disadvantaged and vulnerable pupils. Attachment Theory makes an important contribution to understanding these complex difficulties, enhancing the teacher's repertoire of responses in ways which can 'make a difference'. Such understanding contributes to the emotional health and well-being of all pupils.

Summary and Chapter Structure

- It is clear that children are subject to a wide range of social and emotional experience which affects them to a greater or lesser degree. Behaviour is often a response to distressing experience. Behaviour, which can be provocative, alarming and distressing to others, and which adversely affects learning, can thus be a clue to the child's own distress. In further chapters pupil behaviour and responses to learning will be explored in more detail from the perspective of early experience and Attachment Theory in particular.

- Pupil behaviour will be examined more closely in relation to social and emotional experiences and linked to learning – Chapter 2

- Attachment Theory and the significance of early relationships will be discussed in detail as a factor which profoundly affects vulnerability and resilience – Chapter 3

- A model which links Attachment Theory and learning will be proposed – Chapter 4

- Adverse Attachment experience will be explored in detail in relation to responses to the teacher and to the educational task. Intervention strategies derived from experience will be proposed, relevant to each pattern of behaviour – Chapters 5, 6 and 7

- Teacher support and reflective practice will be discussed as a means of developing and strengthening the capacity of schools to respond more positively to pupil need, indicated by challenging behaviour – Chapter 8

Chapter 2

Behaviour has meaning
A communication about experience

It makes a great deal more sense of much of the seemingly unreasonable or outrageous behaviour of many ... children if one bears in mind that they are often doing to others what they experience as being done to them, both externally and internally   (Boston & Szur 1983, p.3)

Schools are a significant source of health in the community. No matter what policies predominate, most schools represent a concern and care for children which is a sustaining experience for many pupils whose emotional and social needs are not entirely met by family and environment. However, pupils whose pastoral needs cannot be met may be unable to put aside their anxieties and pre-occupations; these may be expressed as behaviour which can interfere with the learning process. Such patterns of behaviour, familiar to all teachers and school staff, can persist in making some pupils increasingly difficult to teach.

In this chapter, the meaning of behaviour is explored, and links are made between social and emotional experience and behavioural difficulties in school. The aim is to introduce those working with children in an education setting, (teachers, school heads, governors, SENCOs, Learning Support Assistants and administrative staff) to the possible meaning of behaviour as a communication about preoccupations and experiences. These insights can serve to broaden the repertoire of understanding about behaviour and so influence interventions.

The range of examples given are largely taken from clinical experience, but are used to illustrate the links, uncovered in the clinical setting, between learning and behaviour. The examples given represent responses to relatively common life events and are likely to be observed in any classroom. Behaviour, and the specific nature of the learning difficulty, are often linked, even though the connection may be obscure. Such links imply that the difficulty in learning can be thought of as a *symptom* of a child's preoccupations and experiences. Uncovering the meaning of the behaviour and making the meaning explicit can release the block on learning, and progress can continue.

It is also possible that pupils bring this behaviour to school in the unconscious hope that someone will understand their needs, and respond by understanding their communication. With their direct day-to-day experience of pupils, teachers and other staff are well placed to be the people who can do this. Without becoming therapists or social workers, school staff can use such insights and understanding to enhance well-being in pupils, and increase access to achievement and social inclusion.

Examples will be given which illustrate how behaviour and learning can be affected by:

- performance fears
- pre-occupations about separations
- the impact of loss
- confusion about numbers
- the effects of traumatic experience
- repressed hostility and reading difficulties
- relationships which affect responses in school.

Examples illustrating the links between behaviour and learning

I believe it is useful to begin by being hopeful, and by acknowledging the impact that good educational practice can have on children whose behaviour may reflect experiences and expectations which have not prepared them for school routines.

It is early in Year 1 and the children have been in this year group for a few weeks. Greater demands are made for pupils to conform to classroom rituals. The children arrive in the classroom and, in various ways, drift to the carpet and sit together looking expectantly towards the teacher.

Allan dashed through the door, crashed into another boy and fell in a heap on the carpet. As the register was called, he nudged those around him, rolled about and made faces and called out. It was difficult for the teacher to retain the class attention when Allan was so disruptive and destructive of her authority. Allan seemed to have little capacity to respond to words and explanations. For many weeks, Allan continued to find arriving and conforming to the teacher's expectations difficult. It is as if he had not experienced an adult with authority and did not seem able to make sense of verbal and social cues.

Later in the year, Allan was spotted in the corridor, sharing the duty of carrying the register to the office in the morning. He was glowing with pride and smiled broadly at me as he passed. Allan had made major adjustments to conforming to school routines and responded to praise and rewards.

This is a familiar story for many children who have not been appropriately prepared for the expectations of school but who, over time, respond to predictable routines and structures and to positive encouragement.

Performance fears

Eight year old Lee had been excluded from his primary school for aggression towards his teacher. In the one-to-one sessions of Home Tuition he was presented with learning tasks to assess his skills. He was articulate and responsive and his mother described his interest in the stories that she read to him. However, it soon became clear that Lee had acquired very few educational skills. He did not know the names of letters, he could read very few words and although he understood counting, he had no strategies for tackling more complex maths tasks. It was as if he did not know how to do things rather than not understand the problem. It transpired that Lee's family had moved around a lot; he had attended several schools, and only recently settled in the local primary school where he soon became noticed for his very aggressive behaviour towards the teacher. He expressed this anger towards the home tutor when a maths task was set which he had no idea how to approach.

Lee's lack of skills caused him great distress. The drawing on the paper (Figure 3) may have been a memory of an earlier angry face, but also expressed his hostility towards the teacher who had not been sensitive to the deficiencies in his educational experience. For several years he had experienced the frustration of 'not knowing how to' in several schools. Careful remedial teaching helped to restore Lee's confidence and supported him in making progress in reading, spelling and maths and settling in a new school place.

Fig. 3 Lee's drawing

For many pupils, performance anxiety can be behind their difficulties and behaviour, and if this is not recognised, patterns of behaviour can persist which exaggerate learning difficulties. Consequently, behaviour becomes the issue rather than the learning need. An assessment of skills is thus a useful exercise when considering behavioural difficulties.

Pre-occupations about separation

A mother was worried about her daughter's behaviour. Ellen (ten) was sad and quiet. The parental couple had recently separated and father lived a long way away. In a story about a wish, Ellen drew a picture of herself on the beach with her cat watching a dolphin playing in the sea. Both were her favourite creatures. She said she didn't know whether to go into the sea to play with the dolphin or stay on the beach with her cat.

The picture seemed to summarise Ellen's dilemma, her conflict of desire, between wanting to stay with mum and wanting to be with dad. Maybe the hope behind this dilemma was that her mother and father could be together again. Putting the wish onto paper made it possible for it to be understood by another who could facilitate the conversation between Ellen and her mother about how much she missed her dad and influenced mother's resistance to dad visiting more frequently.

Ellen's pre-occupation with this conflict was evident in her sad demeanour which was recognised by staff in school and triggered a concern which led to the intervention. A quiet girl was noticed.

A small boy in Year 2 was often distressed in the mornings after he had been brought to school. His anxiety was fuelled by real concerns for his mother after a long experience of abusive partners, refuges and home changes.

He struggled to leave the building and to return home. He often left the class, hiding in the toilet, in corridors and empty spaces. He often responded violently to attempts to hold and to reason with him. On one such occasion, he responded to a suggestion that he might draw a picture to give to his mum later, and he drew a picture of himself, his brothers and their mum, to look after for her until the end of the day. He calmed enough to return to class.

He appeared to be constantly driven to seek reassurance about his mother's safety.

The drive to leave the classroom can often be associated with anxiety about risk in a situation outside school, the physical act of walking out thus serving as a communication about an 'external' concern.

Loss and learning

Seven year old Freddie was becoming increasingly isolated in class. The teacher was desperate about his inability to concentrate on or finish a task. She had decided that he needed to sit alone in order to avoid distractions. But this seemed to trigger his relentless need to move about the classroom even more, defying the teacher's commands to sit alone.

In one-to-one sessions of educational therapy, he demonstrated his need to wander from object to object in the room, handling things but apparently unable to find what he wanted. He suddenly responded to a specific picture in a book, 'Father Christmas Goes on Holiday' (Briggs, 1975). The picture was the poignant moment when Father Christmas packs his car for departure and then says "Goodbye" to his cat and his dog before leaving. Freddie became still, overwhelmed by sadness. At that moment it seemed that he was in touch with his sad experience, two years previously, of saying goodbye to his father who went on a trip and was subsequently killed in a car crash and did not return.

From then on, beginnings and endings of sessions were very sensitive times, and Freddie was able to be angry with the therapist whenever he had to say goodbye. It became possible to talk about his feelings of sadness and anger about his father.

Freddie's difficulties seemed to arise from his unresolved feelings of grief at the sudden loss of his father making it difficult to think, especially when separated from others or to contemplate anything coming to an end. In the presence of the therapist, receptive to his thoughts and the meaning of his behaviour, Freddie's repressed feelings about his lost father were triggered and made explicit. He began to make sense of his own feelings and to contemplate endings.

Sometime later, Freddie was observed sitting outside the classroom, at the quiet table, alone, finishing his work.

Stewart, age eight, and a very vulnerable boy, had recently experienced his mother's sudden death. The classroom assistant began Circle Time by reading 'Badger's Parting Gift' (S. Varleys, 1984). The response from the group about a range of losses demonstrated the universality of endings. Children talked of their lost grannies, absent dads and siblings and Stewart was able to tell the class about his mother dying.

The class seemed to become able to think together about the sadness of loss and to all gain from putting feelings into words, facilitated by an adult who could tolerate their sadness.

On a larger scale, catastrophic events can occur which affect all pupils. In a secondary school, a boy was killed in a tragic accident in the playground. The school planned a programme of rituals, assemblies and commemorative activities to help pupils to grieve the loss of their friend and also provided time and space for all pupils to seek help in a variety of ways across the school.

  A colleague and I sat at a table in the corner of the hall with drawing paper and pencils. Pupils drifted towards the table and began to talk and to draw; about a mum whose baby had died 'before it was born', a grandfather who had suddenly died, a dad who had moved away, the death of several pets and other events where loss and sadness lingered.

One death triggered memories of other losses and the school staff had exercised incredible sensitivity in their response to the event.

Resolving loss can reverberate around families and through generations. Beaumont (1988) describes the implications for learning for the child born following the death of a stillborn baby. Arnold (1977) describes the intergenerational implications of separation and losses resulting from migration of families from the Carribean to Britain.

It is an important aspect of school practice to be sensitive to beginnings and endings, absences and leavings. Plans can be made for significant events, so that tragedy can be thought about and communicated by words and through rituals, so helping to process powerful emotional experience and not to deny it.

Confusing numbers

Phil was fourteen, attending a social services centre for young people at risk, and with no school place. In the morning education class, maths was his Achilles' heel. Numbers 'did his head in', and his rage became threats to 'smash your head in' or 'do a knee-cap job', laced with vivid curses. Yet he wanted to come to the City and Guilds Basic Numeracy Course, as if he really wanted to understand numbers.

At a point where he was helping to write a court report, he was asked about his family. This became an absorbing task, and involved considerable confusion for Phil. His confusion was eased by drawing a family tree, to try to untangle the complex relationships between all the members of his extended family. His father had been married several times, twice to the same person. There were many offspring, some of whom even had the same first name. It took some time to map the relationships and time-scale, and work out who was related to whom and how old each person was. But the outcome was rewarding, since numbers did begin to make sense to Phil, extending to a capacity to become quite philosophical.

Phil's anger at numbers seemed to be related to his anger and confusion about relationships within his family, as if numbers expressed something of his feelings concerning these relationships, a 'something' about which he had been unable to think.

Trauma and thinking

Luke was nine. Two years previously he had witnessed his mother being attacked by her boyfriend. His teacher was very concerned about his inability to carry out the tasks that were set. He focused on presenting meticulous copied writing but with little or no connection to the meaning of the task. He did not seem able to think about what anything meant, only how it looked. He had made little progress in class.

In one-to-one sessions he was extremely uncooperative and appeared to be unable to conform to any of the teacher's expectations. All his attention seemed to be taken up by anxiety about being away from the class and trying to return to the class. It seemed as if being alone in the room with the teacher was persecuting him. I repeatedly wondered aloud if he thought we would be safe enough in the room together, and thought to myself about his experience of not being able to escape from the kitchen in which his mother was being attacked.

He seemed incapable of focusing on any task, and a powerful effect of his behaviour was to make me feel extremely angry. I was fairly certain that the traumatic event was always close by in his mind, but that he was unable to think about it. I despaired of being able to make any difference.

He had steadfastly resisted any creative activity, but on one occasion, he suddenly agreed to draw a picture so that we could begin a story. This coincided with the anniversary of the traumatic event, and may be an example of subtle cues which trigger memory. He drew the only object on the table, a pencil with a rubber on the end. When asked if he could write what it was, he mis-spelled the word 'rubber' as 'robber'. I commented that it was an interesting way to spell rubber because rubber and robber did the same thing – they took something away. He responded quickly by drawing a house on the same page with a mat in front of the door with 'welcome' written on it. He then drew and wrote some more, describing how the robber was able to enter the house whenever he wanted to and leave holding his bag of 'goodies' that he had taken from it. The figures looking on with staring eyes were described as 'sad' and 'mad' (Figure 4). I thought about the possible associations with his experience and the content of the picture: about the 'robber' who was 'welcome' in their house, who harmed his mother and took away the 'goodies'.

I wondered aloud about the children feeling sad and mad but also perhaps feeling helpless and scared and being young and small and not able to stop what happened. Luke was very quiet. He seemed able to stay

Fig. 4 Luke's drawing

with his thoughts for some time and no longer struggled to escape or to resist involvement. The drawing seemed to serve the purpose of putting difficult and hard-to-think-about feelings 'outside', where they could be thought about with someone else who could help to make sense of them. It seemed to be a moment when the trauma of Luke's experience could be revisited and thought about, perhaps for the first time.

Luke attended many sessions after that. He seemed to be able to tolerate my presence and permitted shared experiences of stories and games, making his own games with special rules. His reading ability improved and he was able to co-operate and to understand more about what he was doing in class. He later made a successful transfer to secondary school and continued with support to make progress in learning.

Luke seemed like a boy whose abilities were frozen, a symptom of traumatic response (Moore 1990, Perry 1994, Bentovim 1992). Trauma can have this effect on children; making them appear to 'go stupid' (Sinason 1992, 1995). This extreme form of life event is hopefully rare in ordinary circumstances, but demonstrates the need to be vigilant about children who are unable to learn despite support and interventions.

Unresolved hostility and reading inhibition

Beaumont (1989) associates lack of assertiveness with difficulties in reading. It is as if a certain amount of aggression is required in order to attack and assimilate the words on the page. For Gary, hostility felt towards his mother had become associated with letters and affected his ability to look at words and to read.

> *Gary was seven when he was referred to the clinic for educational therapy. His parents were afraid of his fearsome temper, and at school he seemed remote and odd, making little progress in reading and spelling and very reluctant to write. During sessions, Gary demonstrated a lot of hostility towards me as he elected to play a game, similar to hangman, that he had made up. Whenever I did not guess a letter correctly, his piece moved closer and closer until it blew me up. It was as if letters had special power. He carried on this attack playing board games and showed an almost sadistic glee when I lost. In time he began to draw monsters, and out of this emerged a monster called 'e' monster which was fierce and had sharp teeth (Figure 5).*
>
> *No matter how many other monsters were made up, 'e' always managed*

to defeat them. I felt that Gary was always left with a rage that he could not overcome, possibly associated with his rage at his rather fragile and weak mother. In the metaphor of stories and drawings, this rage was acted out in battles with other monsters. Eventually e.monster was defeated by being cut up each week over and over again until finally it was dead. An enormous collage of monsters was prepared with monsters cut up and mounted which demonstrated the defeat of e.monster. Gary spontaneously wrote sentences which described the battles. During that week, Gary read effortlessly and said "my brain works now the e.monster's gone".

It was as if the rage had been contained by the therapist and the metaphor of the stories, and Gary could use his mind again to think with. For Gary, letters and 'e' in particular had become imbued with the rage he could not express; consequently, words had become dangerous, affecting his capacity to look at words and to read.

Fig. 5 Gary's drawing

A further example is now given which demonstrates how relationships can be a source of difficulties affecting engagement in learning, and that introduces the topic which is the focus of this book.

Relationships and learning

Stan was a twelve/thirteen year old boy referred by school because of attendance problems, lack of any progress in learning, and concern about a recent outburst of aggression at school that was out of character. His mother was concerned about his lack of progress in learning but complained that schools were always focusing on his behaviour instead of his learning problems. Stan had been described, in discussion with his year head, as belligerent and uncooperative. He attended four assessment sessions. On the first occasion both he and his mother came to the treatment room together and mother seemed surprised that Stan would be expected to attend the sessions by himself.

Once within the sessions, I presented Stan with tasks to assess his skills and also projective tasks aimed at understanding his underlying feelings and perceptions. It was immediately evident that Stan was more concerned with challenging the authority of the teacher and subverting the tasks so that they would become more like his choice than mine. It was as if he could not tolerate me having ideas that were not his. His manner was passively resistant, making me feel ignored and de-skilled. He was able to join in the projective tests within which there was more scope for personal control and expression. His first squiggle drawing was to turn a curly line into a snake which he spelled as 'SNAK' (Figure 6).

Fig. 6 Stan's drawing

Stan was very overweight and his mother appeared to have no control over his constant eating; he helped himself from the fridge kept stocked by his mother. Their eating habits seemed to be connected to hostility that was kept at bay by her constant anticipation and gratification of his needs. Perhaps the aggressive snake was kept under control by the incessant 'snack'. In Winnicott's (1971) interpretive framework, perhaps the hostile infant was kept permanently pacified by continuous gratification.

In play situations of free choice, Stan demonstrated considerable intelligence and practical aptitudes. He could calculate but ignored conventional math's practices. He spelled haphazardly. He read well and drew and made complex models, but only if he was in control of the materials and the planning. When other ideas or suggestions were offered he became resistant and aggressive.

The outcome of the assessment was to recognise the nature of Stan's relationship with his mother and the implications of this for learning.

They appeared to be very close, forming a sub-group within the family. Stan exerted considerable control over his mother and could, he said, "get anything he wanted". She seemed to welcome their intimacy as 'special' and despite what teachers at school had been saying, persisted in seeing him as a boy who was struggling to learn but was misunderstood. She did not seem able to see her son as anything but the boy she wanted him to be. This privileged relationship was hard for Stan to give up in order to learn from the teachers in school.

The outcome of this experience, as described by Barrett & Trevitt (1991 p.13), is a child whose needs have been met before he has experienced them, and to whom frustration is unbearable. He does not learn that anger and frustration can be survived or that his wishes are not commands. This results in a child in school for whom the normal frustrations of 'not knowing' are intolerable and the defence of omnipotence is assumed to guard against the awful feelings of helplessness and dependency (see Chapter 6). The teacher is perceived as an attacker who is threatening this state by expecting growth of thinking and knowledge, and independence. Accompanying this is enormous hostility towards the perceived source of the threat, the teacher and the school.

These examples suggest that responses to the expectations of the teacher and to learning can be pre-determined by experiences of early important relationships. This leads to an exploration of Attachment Theory and is the focus of subsequent chapters.

Summary

● These examples relate behaviour, observed and experienced in the classroom, to difficulties in focusing and thinking about the task, when a pupil is preoccupied by unresolved issues from the past or current difficulties. Educational staff are very familiar with these scenarios.

● Linking experience out of school with behaviour inside school can help to make sense of the confusion. Making sense of behaviour protects the teacher from a bombardment which can be demoralizing and exhausting, and enhances pupil resilience and the capacity to think and to learn.

● The aim of focusing on Attachment Theory is to increase the teacher's repertoire of understanding about the meaning of behaviour; in particular, about behaviour as a communication about relationships and expectations. This expanded understanding can inform interventions in the classroom.

● Using the framework of Attachment Theory, the significance of relationships in the classroom will be more closely examined with implications for teaching and learning, beginning with an outline of Attachment Theory and associated research. This will be followed in subsequent chapters by an exploration of pupils' responses to teacher and task, viewed from an attachment perspective (Geddes 1999).

● Reflective workshops, such as those described in Chapter 8, help to hone the skills of understanding behaviour, enabling teachers to develop appropriate responses and strategies. This can contribute to relieving teacher stress, and ultimately, enable pupils to learn and to achieve.

Chapter 3

Outline of Attachment Theory
Why is the teacher important?

In this chapter Attachment Theory will be introduced, together with associated research which identifies patterns of behaviour predisposing children's responses in later life, in particular to relationships and engagement in the outside world. These form the basis for links which are made between early attachment experience and pupil behaviour in school, with particular significance for the expectations of the teacher and engagement in the learning task.

The research links

Sroufe's studies (1985) provide convincing evidence concerning behavioural response in the learning situation. He and his colleagues were able to make distinctions concerning 'qualitatively different patterns of maladaptation' (p.68), and concluded that results 'clearly indicate the importance of the *quality of attachment* as a predictor of behaviour in pre-school' (p.156). Barrett & Trevitt (1991) have laid the foundations for teachers to think about the implications of attachment experience for teaching and learning. They proposed that distorted maternal attachment experience gives rise to problematic behaviour of a specific nature. Johnson (1992) and Williams et al. (1994) have also pointed to the importance of attachment experience in the identification of children at risk in schools, and recommend such knowledge as a tool in further understanding the complex situation of emotional and behavioural difficulties in the school setting. From a detailed study of a sample of cases (Geddes 1999), it was possible to identify specific patterns of response to the teacher and to the educational task, linked to Attachment and life experiences,` with implications for social inclusion.

The most formidable body of research and evidence concerning the nature and quality of early experience, and the implications of early relationships, developed as an outcome of Attachment Theory, which originated with John Bowlby. Because of the importance of this paradigm, it is important to briefly review the theory and research as a precursor to understanding attachment in relation to learning.

Bowlby and the origins of Attachment Theory

Bowlby first developed an interest in the effects on childhood of family experience when he worked for a short time in a progressive school for delinquent boys, and subsequently wrote the article *Forty-four Juvenile Thieves* (1944). He developed a sense of the origins of their difficulties in their unhappy and disrupted childhoods.

He later collaborated with James and Joyce Robertson, and produced a film which documented the distress shown by a small girl when separated from her parents (Robertson1952).

Bowlby was convinced that deprivation of maternal care had long lasting effects. His work for the World Health Organisation (WHO) confirmed this conviction. He found a high degree of agreement about the principles underlying the mental health of children and concluded that if children were separated from their mothers or primary care givers during the first few years of life, lasting psychological damage could result. The ensuing report *Maternal Care and Mental Health* (Bowlby, 1951) described the effects of deprivation of maternal care. This was rewritten as a popularised version, *Child Care and the Growth of Love,* which has been in print since 1952.

This book brought to public attention Bowlby's belief that what was necessary for mental health was that the 'young child should experience a warm, intimate and continuous relationship with his mother' (p.11). He called upon studies of juvenile delinquents, institutionalised children and children in residential nurseries to support the view that maternal deprivation can seriously affect children's emotional, intellectual, social and physical development. An important idea to emerge from Bowlby's work at the time was that of 'cycles of disadvantage', leading to the belief that today's neglected children become tomorrow's neglectful parents.

In the psychoanalytic tradition, theories concerning early emotional development are derived from recall and reconstruction. Bowlby's data were drawn from 'the observation of young children in the real life situation' on the basis that 'the younger the subject, the more likely are his behaviour and mental processes to be two sides of the same coin' (Bowlby 1969, p.6). The first research technique was carefully recorded observation of infant/mother dyads (pairs) (Ainsworth 1967). The original experimental work in this field was by Ainsworth et al (1969). In their research setting known as the Strange Situation Procedure, observations of the nature and quality of interactions between mothers and infants led to further developments in understanding the 'mechanisms' of Attachment, and implications for later sociability.

Social changes have come about informed by Bowlby's work. For example, new babies are no longer separated from their mother at birth, and parents are accommodated in hospital with children needing treatment. The notion of maternal care is a cornerstone of many social policies, and in particular, that of the Sure Start movement, which supports early infant/parent relationships. Subsequently, a greater focus on the experience of a wider range of relationships has facilitated recognition that children are capable of independent relationships with significant others. This adds diversity to early experience, with implications for later outcomes.

The Core Concepts of Attachment Theory

The Secure Base

Bowlby (1988) maintained that all of us, from the cradle to the grave, are happiest when life is organised as a series of excursions, long or short, from the Secure Base provided by our attachment figures.

Human infants are biologically predisposed at birth to seek and make strong emotional bonds with another, and to seek safety in their presence. This occurs with a figure who gradually becomes the significant attachment figure. In the context of this relationship, the infant's survival needs are met in terms of physical requirements for food, warmth and protection. But, in addition, there soon develops a preference for contact and proximity with this person, regardless of basic needs. Absence of the person can trigger alarm, but the infant is soothed on their return.

As the capacity for mobility develops, the infant feels safe to explore, confident in the availability of the Secure Base at times of stress such as tiredness, hunger, discomfort and when startled or afraid.

The 'containing' quality of the Secure Base

The capacity and sensitivity of the mother, and her ability to understand the anxiety triggered by fear and uncertainty, is a significant aspect of early Attachment experience. Bion (1967) has linked this to learning and thinking. Bion's concepts give a conceptual framework for understanding the links between frustration and thinking which have subsequently been described by neuroscientists in terms of brain development (outlined below). However, Bion's concepts remain a very useful framework, and relate to later discussions about pupil behaviour and teacher support.

Bion describes the process whereby the infant, who has no experience of the future or the outside world, experiences needs as overwhelming. The 'sensitive-enough' mother understands her child's desperation and can herself bear the anxious quality of it; she responds in a way that communicates this understanding. Bion names this as 'containment'. The infant is reassured by the mother's understanding response, and his or her anxiety is diminished by the experience of being understood.

In the words of Kate Barrows (1984)

> … the first gift from another person is the maternal gift of taking in his feelings, absorbing them, thinking about them and giving them back to him in a way he can accept.   (p.15)

Emanuel (2000) writes, a baby needs a container to investigate his feelings and to find out what he is feeling and what it means.

As language begins to enter into this experience, words can play a part in diminishing anxiety and fear can be understood by communication and thinking. The whole process involves transforming fear into thinkable thoughts. In this way, the child acquires the capacity to think about fears so that frustrations can be tolerated, mediated by talking and thinking. This mechanism of thinking, when challenged by uncertainty, then becomes available to the baby as a way of coping with future fears alongside an expectation that when the challenge is too great, supportive others will be available to provide a containing function. Without this process, challenge can create anxiety which can feel overwhelming, and can contaminate learning experiences. Contained anxiety can facilitate thinking and learning. Excessive uncertainty can inhibit thinking and learning. The concept of 'containment' of anxiety can also be adapted to institutional practice and the organisation and practices of a school can be experienced as 'containing'. This theme is repeated throughout following chapters related to behaviour and to learning and to whole school thinking, in particular in chapter 8.

Attachment behaviour

In order to maintain a comfortable proximity to the secure base, the infant and mother negotiate a relationship based on the disposition they both bring to the relationship. The quality of the attachment reflects the mother's capacities to recognise and respond to the signals that her infant makes to achieve contact and proximity. They negotiate a way of responding to each other which reflects this. This is described in the infant as *attachment behaviour*. The aim of attachment behaviour is proximity or contact (with the attachment figure), with the associated feelings of security and safety.

Ainsworth (1963) observed that although attachment behaviour was shown towards other familiar adults, it was almost always shown earlier, more strongly and more consistently towards mother. From her observations, she was struck by the extent to which from two months onwards and increasingly through the first year, the infant is not passive but actively seeks interaction.

The quality of the attachment relationship has implications for how the child learns about him/herself and others. It acts as an organiser of behaviour towards others in ways that persist into adult life, affecting later relationships and choices (Sroufe 1983, Grossman & Grossman 1991).

Empathic attunement

The human baby is highly responsive to human interaction. The face is a powerful communicator and triggers emotional responses. The baby is highly susceptible to face-to-face interactions; within the intimate face-to-face relationship between mother and child, the infant makes his/her needs known by overt and subtle communications. A sensitive-enough mother learns to read these signals, and responds appropriately. She soon knows when her child is cold or hot, hungry or tired, wanting her presence or needing a nappy change – the mother understands her baby's feelings (affect).

Importantly, the infant's communications are *translated* by the mother's responsive facial and verbal gestures and actual responses. The cry which expresses a feeling associated with being hungry is met by the response of being fed. Thus the infant learns about its own needs and feelings by the response he/she experiences. The baby learns about him/herself by being understood by another – the basis of empathy.

The maternal response is accompanied by language. Words are associated with the baby's signals and words can then stand for experiences. This happens with particular respect to emotional states and the infant learns that feelings can be recognised, given meaning by being understood and named. This also applies to fear and anxiety. These strong feelings can be transformed into language and thought, by being understood by another, laying the foundations of emotional intelligence.

The mother's sensitivity to the infant's signals is thus at the heart of the infant learning about itself, and, subsequently, about others.

Secure Attachment and the development of the infant's brain

More recent developments in neuroscience have helped to link this early inter-relational experience with the development of the brain (Perry 1994, Moore 1998, Schore 2000, Gerhardt 2004). Children are receptive to experience from the moment the brain begins to develop. Genetic disposition interacts with the environment and the brain develops; neurons begin to link into response pathways.

Change the environment and the development of the brain changes. This remains true throughout life. Connections and pathways develop in response to stimulus and experience and lay the foundations for later responsiveness.

The human baby is highly responsive to human interaction, particularly in the face-to-face interactions which mark early attachment experience. Schore (2000) describes how 'face-to-face' is highly arousing and affect laden. He also describes how smiles and adoring looks actually stimulate the production of biochemicals which help the brain to grow. He goes on to describe the attachment interaction as 'affect synchrony', in other words, the sensitive attunement of the mother/carer to the infant's feelings and experiences. This reverberates with Stern's observations of the infant's capacity to regulate affect or strong feelings, by averting their gaze (Stern 1985).

The richer the experiences of interaction, the more the neural connections grow and the brain becomes more richly networked. The entire period of infancy is dominated by right brain development, which is the seat of sensitivity to affect regulation and the foundations of emotional intelligence. It is where feelings are experienced, and where emotional behaviour and responsiveness to others' cues are processed and developed. It is where, in the context of the relationship between infant and mother, the 'mutual dance of responsiveness' takes place (Gerhardt 2004, p.31).

This has been defined as affective attunement and is the core experience of Secure Attachment. The adult's sensitive attunement to the infant's experience of the environment assists in the regulation of stress. The adult's presence is essential to prevent overwhelming flooding of emotional experience which cannot be processed or contained at this stage of the infant's primitive development. The absence of the secure base as a container and moderator of stress has major implications for the future management of fears and anxieties.

When management of feelings has been moderated, right and left brain functions begin to integrate. There is a shift from right brain dominance towards left brain functioning at about the infant's second year, as linguistic ability develops. The left brain specialises in sequential and verbal processing and higher order operations. It is also where sequencing of events leads to the development of a sense of a continuous narrative based on before, now and after. As feelings can be put into words, the right and left brain become more integrated. The right hemisphere remains associated with unconscious and affect (emotional) processes, and the left hemisphere with concrete conscious processes. This has implications for how stress can be managed in the context of the classroom and the nature of the learning task. Language and thought can moderate anxiety. Activities which engage left brain function can help to moderate over-stimulated right brain function. (This is explored in more detail in Chapter 7 in relation to particular behaviour associated with *Disorganised Attachment*).

Internal Working Models

The outcome of a warm, satisfying experience of early relationships is that children are more likely to have a positive sense of self and more likely to make close and lasting relationships with others (Main & Cassidy 1988). In Bowlby's terms, a person who has experienced a secure attachment

> is likely to possess a representational model of attachment figure(s) as being available, responsive, and helpful and a complementary model of himself as … a potentially loveable and valuable person
>
> (Bowlby 1980, p.242)

and is likely to

> approach the world with confidence and, when faced with potentially alarming situations, is likely to tackle them effectively or to seek help in doing so
>
> (Bowlby 1973, p.208)

This is known as an Internal Working Model with implications for self confidence and expectations when experiencing the challenges of learning.

Within this core experience, the child will also experience the inevitable separation from the primary union and ultimately the loss of the primary figure. The negotiation of attachment, separation and inescapably, loss, are at the heart of human social development. Bowlby claimed that the Attachment relationship is a cornerstone of further psychological and social development and wrote, '… attachment behaviour is held to characterise human beings from the cradle to the grave' (Bowlby 1979, p.129).

Further research into infant Attachment will now be briefly reviewed.

Attachment research and the nature of the Attachment Relationship

An experimental procedure was devised which has become a benchmark in Attachment Theory research. Ainsworth & Wittig (1969) devised this procedure for studying the interplay between the early infant's attachment behaviour and exploratory behaviour in conditions of low and high stress. The Strange Situation Procedure is a series of controlled episodes, involving an infant of about one year old, the infant's mother and a stranger. The experiences are cumulatively more stressful, and provide an opportunity to observe the child's responses to mother as a base for exploration and as a source of comfort and reassurance as the stress increases. Infants explored the contents of the room most vigorously when the mother was present, where the secure base is available. However an intriguing aspect of behaviour was at reunion, following infant and mother separation. At this point, the infants showed markedly different kinds of responses to mother even after a brief three minute separation. It was possible to identify distinct patterns of behaviour between mothers and infants.   'The method captured early differences in behavioural organisation' (Sroufe 1983, p.47) and reflected the infant's experience and expectations of his or her mother's availability.

Most behaviour patterns, identified in this way, reflected a Secure Attachment. Characteristics of secure attachment demonstrate the mother's capacity to understand her infant's distress at her absence and reassure him/her on her return. The infants of a secure attachment can quickly recover their confidence in their 'secure base', and return to their exploration and play.

However, other infant/mother dyads demonstrated an *insecure response*. In these relationships, the mother was insensitive to her child's distress. After the mother's absence, the infant demonstrated uncertainty at her return, with little restoration of confidence. This uncertainty was shown in different ways with marked differences of attachment behaviour. These insecure patterns were found to be consistent over time (Ainsworth 1982) and in a further research procedure called the Adult Attachment Interview (Main et al 1985), were identified in adulthood.

Patterns of attachment behaviour in response to the teacher and to the task form the cornerstone of profiles of pupil behaviour in the classroom (Geddes 1999). This has major implications for learning and teaching and is the core concept of this book. These patterns of attachment in relation to learning and teaching are described and discussed fully in later chapters.

The experience of secure attachment is explored further here using an example from clinical practice. This helps to understand the experience of insecure attachment which is later described in detail, in terms of responses in school.

Temporary loss of the secure base

Jason, aged five, cried continuously at school but was described as 'OK' at home. His mother described their experience of Jason's father leaving the family. Jason's mother was clearly devastated by the experience which was still fairly recent. Meanwhile, as his mother talked of her distress, Jason made a robot out of the plastic parts. He drew a plan of how the bits fitted together and called it Bendy – the robot who could do anything.

This was interpreted as Jason's need to cope during his mother's state of preoccupation, perhaps only expressing his own grief and worry at school. Subsequently Jason described and drew a 'bad' dream about his ship sinking and being eaten up by the monster who had sunk the ship. He said that he no longer felt he 'could do anything'. This was understood as his experience of losing his father and subsequently his mother's support when he needed it most. His secure base was sunk at a time of great need and distress.

Jason's mother immediately understood how he had coped by looking after himself during her emotional preoccupation. She responded very sympathetically. Jason went over to his mother, sank onto his small chair beside her, and said "I can be a little boy again". It was a poignant expression of Jason's experience of the loss of his secure base and his coping strategies but also of his relief that he could rely on her again.

Jason clearly demonstrates the outcomes of secure attachment. He had derived sufficient resilience and ego strength to 'cope' in the temporary absence of his 'secure base'. Jason also demonstrated abilities to communicate his experience and feelings eloquently with toys, drawings and with ideas and words. The benefits of secure attachment in terms of the capacity to communicate are linked to the experience of his own communications being understood appropriately.

Secure Attachment in school

The most convincing evidence concerning links between attachment experience and children's disposition towards learning has arisen from research described by Sroufe (1983, 1986). It was observed that in a pre-school sample, children who had experienced secure maternal attachment were 'doing well as pre-school children' (p.59). This involved high scores on ego-resilience and self esteem, less dependency on the teacher but with more positive affect towards the teacher. Children who were securely attached infants were 'involved with the teachers' (p.61). They also showed more positive interactions socially. Teachers found such children to be more co-operative and less likely to be management problems. The securely attached children clearly demonstrated a capacity to adapt to school and to respond to the demands of the academic and social setting in which learning takes place.

Waters et al (1979) observed three-and-a-half-year old children in nursery who had been classified as Securely Attached at fifteen months. They were found to be more competent socially, more effective in play, more curious and more sympathetic to others. They concluded that the secure pattern had become a function of the child and was no longer dependent on mother's presence. Arend et al (1979) found patterns to be consistent at five/six years of age with securely attached children demonstrating greater ego strength. In a sample derived from a more deprived population, securely attached infants were reported to be more sociable as toddlers, more compliant at two with mothers and at four-and-a-half with pre-school teachers (Erickson et al 1982), to have better self control in the pre-school (Engeland 1983) and to be less dependent on the pre-school teacher (Sroufe 1983).

Fonagy et al (1993) described the nature of secure parenting which is thought to reflect, predominantly, an experience of relationships with parental figures who were able to permit and support autonomous development of a separate self without contamination by their own unresolved issues. As a result, the child's working model of adult relationships permits uncontaminated relationships with potentially helpful adults such as the teacher (Barrett & Trevitt 1991).

The experience of the insecurely attached child contrasts with this experience in terms of responses to challenge and adversity.

Insecure attachment in school

For most children, early attachment results in a 'good enough' experience, and enables development of a sense of self and expectation of the world which is relatively hopeful and reliable. But when the child's needs for sensitivity to its signals, comfort and reassurance are not met, then insecure attachment can result.

> In homes where the baby finds no mutuality, where the parent's face does
> not reflect the baby's experience and where the child's spontaneous gesture
> is not recognised or appreciated, neither trust in others nor confidence in
> the self develop.   (Hopkins 1990)

The experience of this can be meliorated by other attachment figures so the degree of adversity or of 'anxious attachment' is not necessarily determined entirely by the primary relationship. However, adverse experience of early attachment not relieved by more positive relationships with others is very likely to have negative implications for both behaviour and learning.

Sroufe's work indicated that children who experience insecure attachment respond to challenge with less confidence and face adversity with greater uncertainty than securely attached children. Sroufe (1983) and Erickson et al (1985) observed children in a pre-school programme, involving the teachers in direct interactional observation with the children. The aim was 'to test the hypothesis that children who were anxiously attached would be more likely to have behaviour problems in pre-school and to determine if the particular pattern of anxious attachment related to specific problem behaviours in the pre-school' (p.150).

They found that in general, 'children with a history of anxious attachment are less ego-resilient (have lower self esteem), and are more dependent, show more negative affect and negative behavioural signs, show less positive affective engagement with others and are less popular with peers. In general, they are emotionally less healthy than children with a history of secure attachment' (Sroufe 1983, p.64). It was concluded that the results 'clearly indicate the importance of quality of attachment as a predictor of behaviour in pre-school' (Erickson et al 1985, p.156). The studies described by Sroufe (1983) and Erickson et al (1985), remain the most convincing evidence concerning the response in terms of behavioural organisation in the learning situation.

In the school setting, Barrett & Trevitt (1991) see the teacher as the 'specific attachment person', especially for anxious children. This is particularly applicable when describing the role of a teacher who can represent a 'secure base' in the often confusing and demanding world of school. They constructed graphic models of attachment experience and relate this to behaviour in the learning situation. They quote from Ainsworth et al (1969), 'The less secure child may have so much uncertainty about the availability of the attachment figure that he is preoccupied with keeping proximity to the detriment of exploratory activity'.

Johnson (1992) and Williams et al (1994) suggest that attachment experience has implications for those seeking to assist children in the learning process. Johnson further suggests that knowledge of attachment behaviour assists in the identification of children at risk in schools.

That attachment theory does in fact make distinct classifications of behavioural organisations that may affect a child's ability to adapt in the school setting and inhibit cognitive learning, is of extreme importance in identification of children at risk.   (p.181)

Williams et al (1994) see such knowledge as a tool in helping to untangle the complex behavioural problems that can confuse learning issues. These comments emphasise the importance of understanding insecure attachment experience in terms of classroom behaviour.

Patterns of Insecure Attachment

Three major categories of Insecure Attachment behaviour were identified by the Strange Situation procedure (Ainsworth et al 1978), two of which were described as Organised patterns of behaviour, describing the infant's response to a particular pattern of sensitivity of the parent. The third category appeared to show little consistency or pattern of response, and was described as Disorganised.

Organised Attachment patterns:
- the **Avoidant** pattern   *presented in Chapter 5*
- the **Resistant/Ambivalent** pattern   *presented in Chapter 6*

and the

Disorganised Attachment pattern   *presented in Chapter 7*

Summary

- Bowlby's Theory of Attachment has led to the development of a major developmental paradigm for understanding infant experience in terms of relatedness and its implications for relating and responses in later life.

- The patterns of Attachment behaviour identified by research are laid down in infancy, but are moderated by later experience of other significant relationships which may meliorate adversity experienced in the primary relationships.

- However, for many children, patterns of expectation of self and of others continue to influence behaviour with implications for learning. This will be the focus of subsequent chapters.

Chapter 4

The Learning Triangle
How relationships affect learning

From the material presented, it has been argued that social and emotional experiences affect behaviour in school, and can have specific implications for learning.

Common sense and research both tell us that early experiences of relationships and life events affect our responses, expectations and predisposition to experiences in later life. This also applies to learning.

Attachment Theory and subsequent research tells us the nature of a close and significant relationship in early infancy is a crucial factor in shaping pupil response to learning.

At this point, it is useful to transform the Attachment framework of interpersonal interactions into a model which relates attachment to learning. Research indicates that the pupil of a secure attachment is able to relate to the teacher as well as to others, and finds the world outside the primary relationship worth exploring. The educational experience involves a capacity to relate to the teacher and the presence of the educational task, which implies challenge and the uncertainty of 'not knowing something'. In the learning situation, relationships, tolerance of uncertainty and the task are related.

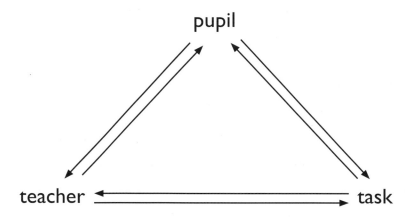

Fig. 7 The Learning Triangle

Beginnings of learning

From an Attachment perspective, the infant's primary experience is in a one-to-one interaction with the significant carer, involving intimate and mutually-involving activities which ensure a reliable bonding. In a short while, it becomes possible for the infant to disengage from this interaction to become interested in objects and activities often introduced by mother or others. This shift of focus takes place in the space between infant and carer where the infant can experience disengagement from the carer without actual separation (Winnicott 1964, p146).

The infant will watch objects held in front of it and reach for them. As mobility increases, the infant will lean towards objects and actively try to make contact with them. He or she will then begin to explore the objects of interest, usually with his or her mouth at first, and then through sight, sound, movement and touching, all of which cause further interest-provoking things to happen. The infant has begun to explore objects in the immediate world within the secure base of the primary attachment relationship, with the experience that the exploration enhances and excites further interest.

This exploration may be accompanied by uncertainty, and perhaps even fear as the unexpected happens. The capacity of the mother to reassure, and to encourage exploration to continue, enables the infant to experience his or her uncertainty being understood and transformed into appropriate responses which 'contain' the anxiety and put feelings into words (Bion 1967). The words then become a source of reassurance and can support exploration from a greater and greater distance. As confidence in the secure base becomes an internalized process, then exploration and experience in the wider world is possible. Experience builds up a repertoire of 'knowledge' about what happens. The satisfaction of this interest leads to additional curiosity and exploration, and the pattern of engaging with and finding out is laid down. This is often supported by interactions with others, but is usually initially promoted by mother.

Play and learning

In this sense, engagement with objects in the outside world begins with play in the presence of a reliable trusted person. The capacity to engage with external objects with curiosity and creativity is the source of the capacity to engage in learning. Such engagement can include playing with object or materials to explore their potential, playing with something unknown until it is understood, making up a situation to see what might happen, listening to others to understand what they might mean, listening to a story to find out what happens. In each of these situations, it is necessary to tolerate the frustration and uncertainty of *not knowing* until something becomes understood. This reflects the early availability of the 'secure base' as a source of 'containment' of anxiety during exploration. As the known increases, so the pupil experiences knowledge and agency as his/her own – a mind of one's own. This is the experience that the pupil brings to the educational task and the nature of this experience is likely to affect engagement.

The uncertainty of not knowing

For some pupils, this experience of a 'containing mind' which reassures and supports and moderates right brain affect with words and assurance, is relatively absent. Uncertainty can be felt as overwhelming anxiety, and tolerating the uncertainty of not knowing becomes an unbearable threat.

Uncertainty about what comes next

Ten year old Carol began to read 'Amos and Boris' (Steig 1971). It is a story about a whale and a mouse. The mouse, Amos, becomes dependent on Boris the whale to save his life at sea. Then Boris the whale becomes dependent on Amos the mouse, to save his life when he is stranded on land. They then have to say goodbye and leave each other knowing they will never meet again. It is a story about attachment, containment, separation and loss.

Carol listened to the page read by the therapist then read her page. She scanned the page with eyes darting about. She flicked the pages forwards to quickly scan the next pictures to get a clue about what was coming next. Her reading reflected this. As she glanced at the pages, she quickly guessed the meaning of words and stumbled through sentences in an incoherent manner, sticking words together with little sense of meaning. It was as if Carol's uncertainty about what might happen next undermined her capacity to think about what was happening now.

Her class teacher commented that she seemed to understand something one minute, and then appeared to have forgotten what she had just known. I wondered if Carol could bear to remain focused on one thing, because the uncertainty about what was coming next was too alarming.

Carol's family had experienced a series of losses over the years causing distress to and pre-occupying her mother. Significant deaths were unresolved. Perhaps Carol had experienced interrupted attention and uncertainty about her mother's emotional presence and availability. Carol's approach to learning may have reflected an experience of an attachment figure who was not consistently available to contain her anxiety when it was aroused, and she did not seem able to permit reliance on the teacher to support her and understand her uncertainty.

The example above stands in contrast to the experience of reading the same story with relatively securely attached children. Such children await the next page with excitement. They nestle closer to the adult at exciting moments, reassured by contact whilst waiting to find out what happens next, confident perhaps that their worries will be understood, their anxiety about uncertainty will be contained. They can bear to talk and think about what might happen next without being overwhelmed by the uncertainty of not knowing. They reflect an experience of contained anxiety and a capacity to continue thinking in the face of uncertainty – an expression of resilience.

The Learning task

In the classroom, the educational task is a critical part of the learning experience and is the location of this activity and process. The teacher sets up the educational task and engages the pupil in finding out about something as yet unknown or not understood. The teacher's skill lies in knowing how to make this knowledge and experience available to pupils whilst engaging their capacities to be curious and to want to find out. The task is located in the transitional space between the teacher and the external world – the classroom. Engaging with the task involves trusting the teacher to support uncertainty and to resolve confusion, within a safe place. The teacher and the classroom come to represent the educational Secure Base.

For a child with a secure attachment experience of sensitive, reliable and trusted adults, the teacher becomes imbued with the expectation that s/he will be helpful and available. Frustrations experienced in the task will be tolerable, and the knowledge gained will be of interest and value. The pupil can turn to the teacher when uncertain and be reassured enough to continue the engagement with the task with increasing independence and autonomy. This pattern of behaviour implies a Secure Attachment experience. The learning triangle for a securely attached child would thus be balanced between the needs of the pupil, the presence of the teacher and the demands of the task. The teacher's sensitivity and skill will usually mean that the task is sufficiently do-able and sufficiently challenging to excite engagement and interest with some but not overwhelming anxiety, resulting in the satisfactory outcome of knowing something that was not known before.

The outcome for the pupil is a sense of efficacy and self-worth, and a capacity to feel able to endure frustration, challenge and uncertainty; in particular, the ability to develop a mind of his/her own – a sense of personal agency. A significant outcome of successful engagement with the educational task is thus enhanced resilience.

In this way the pupil, the teacher and the task are related, as the three participants in the learning process. I describe these relationships as the 'Learning Triangle' which is charged with the potential for emotional and cognitive resilience.

The Learning Triangle of the Securely Attached Pupil

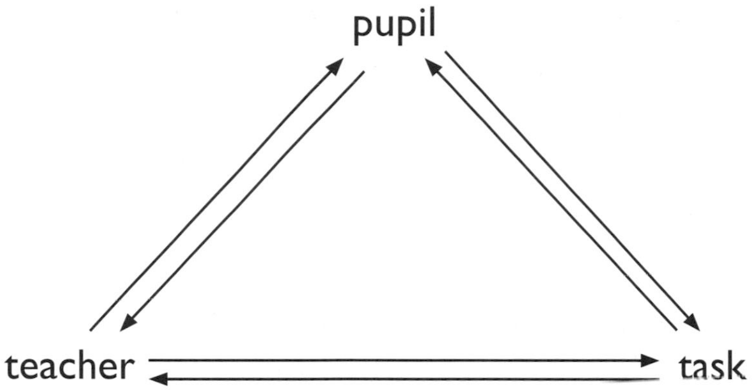

Fig. 8 Learning Triangle: Secure Attachment

For the young pupil of a secure enough attachment, the balance of this relationship reflects a fluid dynamic between engagement and support with the teacher, and involvement in the task. As the child gets older, the presence of the teacher remains but reliance and support diminishes, so that in later school years, pupils can be more self reliant and independent of the teacher, and 'learn for themselves'. This also reflects the pupils' growing emotional and social development, and transition into the adult world.

Insecure attachment patterns introduced earlier (Chapter 3) and explored more fully in later chapters, indicate a distorted version of the Learning Triangle. This reflects a different expectation of the teacher and response to the task, imbued by the pupil with their own Attachment experience.

School as a Secure Base

There is thus the potential to replicate 'secure' experience in the practices and responses of a school. A whole school staff, head, govenors, SENCo, teachers and all support staff, who are united in promoting the well-being of all pupils, provide a framework in which the pupil can experience a reliable and secure base. Within this, the teacher's sensitivity to the pupil's uncertainty and a task which facilitates interest and engagement can enhance the pupil's positive sense of self.

School as an insecure base

As has been stated, the pressure on schools and on teachers to focus on measurement and comparisons of performance can obscure the emotional and interpersonal experience at the heart of teaching and learning. Teachers can become preoccupied by performance and content, which can inhibit their capacity to focus on the emotional experience of learning. This can have a negative effect on school experience for pupils who may have experienced an adverse early relationship in which their needs may have been overlooked because of parental preoccupations or external pressures.

School systems can thus replicate insecurity when the focus of their intentions ignores the emotional experience of pupils. In such a climate, disaffected peer groups can grow which collude in denying the importance of learning – 'where it is not cool to be clever' (Phillips, The Guardian, London 7th March 2005).

I recall my own experience of being a pupil in a primary classroom in the far-off days of the early 1950s. The poorest performing pupils sat in the 'low row'. The class was preparing for the 11+ examination for selection for the available places in the local grammar school. The pupils in the 'low row' struggled. One girl could not read and sat dumbly through most lessons with occasional reading help from a girl in the 'top row'. One boy wet himself regularly and sat in smelly embarrassment. One boy wrote backwards and always seemed bewildered. Others also struggled and experienced the humiliation of the teacher deriding their capacity to keep up and to understand the lessons. In the assembly where the 11+ results were read out in front of the whole school, the pupils from the 'low row' sat quietly accepting their fate of limited opportunities whilst others more fortunate and more able to learn were singled out to perform and shine elsewhere.

This rather archaic example, from days of much greater repression of feelings and reactions, makes the point that systems which identify academic success as the only hallmark of educational success are potentially very damaging. Times have certainly changed and there is a far greater equality of opportunity implied in current practice. However, the hysteria produced by starred A level results can feel very disheartening to vulnerable pupils whose academic needs and capacities are not recognised with the same degree of respect and interest. Schools identified publicly as 'failing' can be discouraging to those who have little choice in where they attend. Humiliation can be a trigger for powerful defensive behaviours, involving anger and disaffection.

Within an educational climate in which there is a preoccupation about performance, achievement and league tables, this can be experienced as less concern for the emotional well-being of pupils, and can replicate insecure attachment experiences.

Fathers and learning

The triangular nature of the learning relationship implies that the child can tolerate an intrusion into the primary relationship between child and 'mother' related here to the pupil's capacity to tolerate the presence of the educational task. It is a Freudian concept that the child needs to learn to bear the presence of 'another' in the primary dyad (of mother and child); this is the intrusion/inclusion of 'father'. Freud (1989) describes the primitive conflict as the child negotiates this readjustment of his 'ownership' of mother (the so-called Oedipal conflict). In this sense, the pupil's response to engagement in the outside world of infant and mother may reflect the quality of resolution of this challenge. Beaumont identifies the paternal significance of the learning task and quotes Britton et al (1989) '… until he (the child) can tolerate the position of 'being a witness (to his parents' relationship) and not a participant, he is going to remain inextricably merged with his mother' (Beaumont 1991, p.262).

This psychoanalytic perspective suggests that relationships with fathers can play a significant role in the child's developing capacity to engage with the outside world.

Steele (2002) writes, 'reports from longitudinal studies of mothers, fathers and their children point to inner world emotional lessons 'taught' by mother and more outer world social lessons 'taught' by father'. Other research also associates paternal influence with 'outer world experiences' (Suess et al 1992 and Verschueren & Marcoen (1999). Karen (1998) describes the importance of the relationship between boys and fathers; 'both the quality of the father's life and the quality of his relationship with his son will deeply affect the developing boy's sense of self and possibilities' (p.199). In a controversial comment made in The Guardian (London, 7th May 2005), Trevor Phillips (Commission for Racial Equality) challenged black fathers to participate more in their children's education linking this to the relatively poor performance of black boys in terms of GCSE results.

An extension of this notion is the comparison of the educational task with its paternal association to the social context and the capacity to be employed in work in the outside world. Freud (1989) proposed the view that mature mental health is reflected by the capacity to love and to work; to engage in relationships and in the social and economic aspects of living in society. It is proposed here that the successful involvement and engagement of 'father' in early emotional experience may be a factor which facilitates engagement in the learning task, and so makes a significant contribution to social inclusion. This comment could be applied to all parental relationships and perhaps encourage absent fathers to recognise their importance. This may have implications for the many children who live in single parent families who

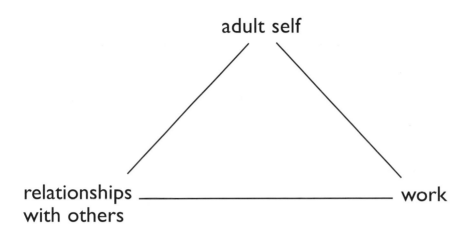

Fig. 9 The Learning Triangle in the social context

also make up half of the families living in poverty. (Financial Times 23rd April 2005)

The Learning Triangle described earlier could thus be used to define later experience in the social context (Figure 9). In this way it is possible to think of engagement in learning, in the educational task, as a precursor to engagement in work and social life. The capacity to access opportunity in terms of later social inclusion may have its roots in the same experiences which can inhibit learning – Attachment relationships.

Summary

- For children of insecure attachment experience, adversity can be meliorated by relationships with other significant carers. Fathers, siblings, grandparents, relatives and friends can offer more positive experiences which will enhance esteem and resilience. In this way, the political climate and community also contribute to the overall well-being of children.

- However, schools in particular are a potent source of emotional

cont.../

well-being and resilience (DfES 2004). Children attend schools for a very long period of their lives, and within it they experience long term relationships with adults. This offers the potential for children to experience themselves more positively, and to experience learning. From this, they gain a sense of agency and involvement in the context of a social group, a rehearsal for later life.

- For many children, school is the access route to achievement and can compensate to some degree for absences in early experiences which inhibit development and learning. It is thus useful to reflect upon the possibilities of enhancing the capacity of School as a Secure Base, and this follows in Chapter 8.

- For the pupil of an insecure early attachment the balance in the relationship between pupil, teacher and the task can be disturbed by experiences which affect the expectations of the teacher and engagement with the task/external world. This is related here to the nature and quality of the early attachment relationship and to anxious attachment behaviour.

- The implications of insecure attachment experience will now be examined in detail and related to a pupil's response to learning in terms of relationships with the teacher and responses to the learning task. Chapters 5, 6 and 7 will closely examine the range of attachment patterns which can arise in infancy, and relate this to the nature of engagement in learning.

Part 2

Linking attachment and learning

As described in Chapter 3 and discussed in relation to learning in Chapter 4, experiences of relationships in infancy can affect expectations and responses in later life. An understanding of the nature of early experience will help to deepen our understanding of the meaning of children's behaviour in school and indicate what kind of response and intervention may be effective. Some children will have been seriously affected by problematic early relationships, and their behaviour will clearly demonstrate their difficulties in particular ways. Others may have experienced other significant relationships which have helped to ameliorate earlier adversity, and their behaviour may be of less concern. There is thus a continuum of responses, and pupils with similar early experiences of attachment may be of greater or lesser concern by the time they enter school. The pattern of response to adults and to learning is likely to demonstrate characteristics reflecting early Attachment experience.

In the following chapters, Attachment behaviour patterns will be presented and described in some detail in terms of:

▲ **Characteristics of the Attachment pattern**s
▲ **How the child might feel** and experience him/herself in
    relation to others
▲ **Examples from practice**
▲ **Implications for learning** described in the **Learning**
    Profile and **Learning Triangle.** These summarise the
    responses of pupils associated with a particular Attachment pattern
▲ **Interventions** which may assist practice

Chapter 5

Pupils who can't ask for help
Avoidant Attachment in the classroom

The 'Avoidant' pupil in school

I quietly entered the Year 5 classroom seeking my next appointment. A slight ripple went round the room as I intruded into the business of the lesson. Faces turned towards me with a variety of reactions. Mary looked directly at me, and said "Take me Miss". I smiled in reply, acknowledging her wish to be noticed and special. Some children were comfortable with the intrusion and simply glanced to see who it was, and reassured that it was nothing very interesting, got on with the task. Others sought some recognition and acknowledgement with a glance, smile or nod. But there were also those who ignored me in a rather conspicuous way, avoiding eye contact and staring downwards at the table. They seemed to be aware of my presence but did not want to acknowledge me.

These pupils remind me of many children who are very sensitive to the presence of someone, but for whom contact with a person triggers uncertainty and is to be avoided. It is such behaviour that is examined now in greater detail in terms of how this pattern of response to relationships develops and how this affects behaviour and learning at school.

CHARACTERISTICS OF AVOIDANT ATTACHMENT BEHAVIOUR

In the sample of infants observed in the Strange Situation, (Ainsworth et al 1978) video film caught the infant and mother responses vividly. Some of the infants showed little or no distress in the separation episodes when mother left the room. When she returned, the infants tended to ignore or avoid contact, proximity or even interaction with mother. They responded reluctantly to mother's coaxing. The mothers were observed to be less sensitive to their babies, somewhat neglectful of their emotional needs and were described as displaying a 'rejection syndrome'. This was associated with the mother's tendency towards 'rejection of physical contact with the infant' and a tendency towards being angry (Main & Weston 1982, p.32). The children developed a particular pattern of behaviour in response to their mother's style of availability. The name *Avoidant* was given to this group because of the tendency to avoid contact with mother rather than seek contact, when anxiety was aroused.

HOW THE CHILD MIGHT FEEL

The conflict expressed by the Avoidant group babies is complex. Like all infants they want close bodily contact at times of distress when feelings of fear or uncertainty are aroused and the attachment system is activated. However, they have also come to avoid closeness with their mother because of the rejection they have experienced. They have a classic approach-avoidance conflict, as quoted from Main (1986) in Hopkins (1987):

> The situation is irresolvable because rejection by an established attachment
> figure activates simultaneous and contradictory impulses both to withdraw
> and to approach. The infant cannot approach because of the parent's
> rejection and cannot withdraw because of its own attachment. The

situation is self-perpetuating because rebuff heightens alarm and hence heightens attachment, leading to increased rebuff, increased alarm, and increased heightening of attachment … In other words by repelling the infant the mother simultaneously attracts him' (p.7-8)

In longer term studies of this attachment group, the children were described as hostile, socially isolated and/or disconnected (Erickson et al 1982).

Clinical description adds to an understanding of the infant's dilemma. Rejection is seen to have a profound effect. They can experience an acute conflict between the 'desire for and the dread of physical acceptance, and a self-representation of being in some ways untouchable or repellent' (Hopkins 1987, p.21). This reflects Bowlby's comment. He described the 'unwanted child' as 'likely not only to feel unwanted by his parents but to believe he is essentially unwantable' (Bowlby 1973, p.204). There is a tendency to fear dependency and neediness and to adopt self-reliance as a defence. In his discussion of 'fear' in relation to separation, Bowlby comments that when a child is afraid of some external object or situation, what he is really afraid of is the absence of someone he needs (p.171). The child of this avoidant pattern whose defence is fearlessness, tends to deny their need for the loved one/secure base.

Bowlby (1973) also associated separations with the arousal of anxiety and anger. Anxiety results from trying to maintain the appropriate proximity and anger is aroused as a reproach against the 'absence' of the attachment figure. He goes on to say that love, anxiety and anger are aroused by the same person resulting in painful conflict (p.235). Prolonged and repeated separations have a double effect of arousing anger and attenuating love. The attachment can then shift from strongly rooted affection laced with 'hot displeasure' (p.249) to a deep running resentment held only partially in check by anxious uncertain affection.

In the follow-up studies of this attachment group, Erickson et al (1985) describe such children as carrying 'an underlying anger that he or she has not learned to express directly' (p.149). Sroufe (1983) had also noted that the avoidant child demonstrated an underlying anger that he has not learned to direct at the source (p.52), in other words the mother. Such angry feelings tend to be directed at objects or others accompanied by more subtle non-compliance (Sroufe 1983, p.49, Bretherton & Waters 1985, p.154). A Kleinian interpretation would be that the child is unable to associate strong negative feelings with the primary object (the mother/carer). Instead, unwanted strong feelings are 'split off' and 'projected' into objects or another person, preserving the belief in the love of the primary object (Klein, Collected Works 1980, Holmes 1993). In this way, anger can often be provoked in others but not felt by the person who is angry. The implications of this are important for the classroom and for the school in general. Teachers and others working with children can often find themselves feeling angry towards certain pupils with no real sense of why. (This is discussed further in Chapter 8).

Holmes (1993) sums up the source and affect associated with Avoidant Attachment:

It seems possible that because these parents have not been able to deal with … their own distress, they cannot cope with pain and anger in their infants and so the cycle is perpetuated. The infant is faced with parents who, due to their own internal conflicts or ego weakness, cannot hold … the child's negative feelings or distress or fear of disintegration. The child is therefore forced to resort to primitive defence mechanisms in order to keep affect within manageable limits. Aggressive feelings may be repressed or split off as in the avoidant child who does not react to the mother's absence but then shows overt aggression towards toys or siblings.   (p.117)

The meaning of avoidance as a function of attachment behaviour was explored by Main & Weston (1982) who suggested that paradoxically, avoidance may function to permit the partners to maintain proximity. The psychological interpretation was that avoidance may be a way of moderating the bearable level of interaction within the dyad; the infant employs avoidance as an alternative to anger felt towards the mother, anger which would otherwise be psychologically intolerable. This moderating function is somewhat like the observations that Stern (1985) described between the very young infant and the mother, with the infant averting its gaze as a way of regulating the level of stimulation given by mother. This suggests that avoidance is a way of preserving organisation which otherwise might result in the child being overwhelmed by extreme anger or distress (Bowlby 1973, Main & Weston 1982). The avoidant adaptation can range from a self-contained and emotionally distant personality approved of in many situations; the British 'stiff upper lip' to the severely schizoid or autistic. At the moderate and less severe end of the Avoidant continuum this may be admired as apparent independence and self reliance, often valued in the classroom.

This pattern of relating would predict an active avoidance of all reminders of mother during her absence. This is reflected in the pupil/teacher relationship and Saltzberger-Wittenberg et al. (1983) suggest that children form important relationships with teachers which are 'imbued with meaning'. This is echoed by Barrett & Trevitt (1991) and evident for pupils such as Barry.

Examples from practice

Barry was observed over a long period of time in a small Year 8 class in a school for pupils with emotional and behavioural difficulties. He had a quiet, intense demeanour and although small and slight was feared by other boys. He had a rather deprived and underfed look with some skin sensitivity. He seemed like a boy who was hungry for something but would be sensitive to being touched.

He entered the classroom with no acknowledgement of the teacher and took his seat. He took out the relevant work materials and proceeded to work on tasks in the maths book carrying on from where he left off in previous lessons. If he encountered a difficulty he closed the book and got another in the series and carried on in this manner. At no time did he ask for help if he did not know how to do something.

In English lessons he read in the round without expression or apparent interest in the content and answered questions with mechanical answers which were not embellished with ideas or reflection.

When he drew, he tended to copy rather than create his own images. He was especially interested in fierce wild animals which made me wonder about his own fierce feelings. His thinking seemed mechanical and concrete and he appeared to avoid activities where feelings and emotion might be expressed. His verbal expressiveness was very limited as if it was dangerous to speak in case too much was said.

On one occasion, the teacher wrote a quiz for the class to cover for a particular lesson. This was a break from routine and outside the usual practice of text book learning. Barry quickly became confused by the questions which were meant to entertain and puzzle. He tore up the quiz and said that it was 'shit' and walked out of the room. His anger and frustration, possibly felt towards the teacher for presenting the challenge and triggering his need to be helped, was directed at the task. I wondered too about his own sense of 'feeling like shit' which many children demonstrate when unable to achieve the task. Tearing up of work as 'rubbish' often feels like an expression of what the child feels about themselves.

It is likely that Barry's response to me, the teacher, was imbued with strong feelings of uncertainty about my availability. I felt as if he was fitted with a proximity meter which enabled him to keep a perfectly judged distance from me. Not too close to trigger his longing for closeness and not too far away to trigger anxieties.

Importance of the task as link

Aware of the possible attachment implications of Barry's responses to the teacher and his sensitivity to my presence, the task became the link between the teacher and Barry. He could become very involved in the task providing he could be autonomous and self-correcting. The writing project was about Aliens. This topic seemed to reverberate with the feelings in the class as they teased and accused each other of being 'weird', 'different', 'odd'. The writing task was differentiated so that whilst working within set objectives there were choices which Barry could make. This proved to be very successful. Barry engaged in more creative work in English resulting in an illustrated story about an alien landing and meeting an Earth boy. They became friends. The picture he drew was colourful and descriptive. He later wrote a children's book criticism which was read out in assembly. Interestingly he chose to critique 'Where the Wild Thing Are' (Sendak 1967). This story is about a boy who is angry with his mother and dreams of monsters. He gains control of the monsters as if gaining control of his fierce feelings towards his mother. There is a touching reconciliation with his mother when he realises that she has left out his supper for him and it is still warm.

In other subjects the same positive outcomes were possible when the focus was clearly on the task and not on the relationship between Barry and the teacher. In this way it was possible to be sensitive to his fear of proximity and need for support but through the safety of the task. This conveys a sensitivity to Barry's needs in contrast to the often hostile response that such covertly angry boys can provoke in adults; a reflective rather than a reactive response.

Gradually, Barry became less hostile and was able to become more expressive and creative and took pride in some of his achievements. He offered to help me to present materials in an assembly about Astronomy. He asked me to help him paint the large cardboard model he had made in art lessons. He could use language to elicit support rather than to abuse and alienate.

His conflict between love and anger began to slip out. In a game of draughts he had me defeated and unable to move. The other boys encouraged him to 'kill her off', 'wipe her out' but Barry walked away from the board unable to ' kill me off'. Later, at Christmas time, he made a card for his mother in which he wrote, 'I love you'. He then added, almost by slip of pen, 'not' so that the message read 'I love you not'. I commented on the message being sent to his mother and he quickly covered up the 'not' with a drawing of a Xmas present tied with a knot. A subtle expression of his conflict – hostility disguised as a gift.

Barry continued to be a distant boy but his capacity to bear the teacher's interest in his ideas and work changed suggesting that over time, the task can be a bridge which links the teacher and pupil rather than separates them. Across this bridge, the pupil experiences reliable interest and concern without feeling threatened by overwhelming feelings. Barry could in time 'relate' more successfully to the teacher and expand his repertoire of experience; his performance improved. In particular his use of language improved in ways which enabled him to share thoughts and ideas about the task, rather than just to mediate distance.

Barry represented an example of Avoidant characteristics, probably at the severe end of the Avoidant continuum. At the more moderate end of the continuum, and more familiar in mainstream classrooms, is Joe. He was referred because of concerns about his withdrawn and distant manner. He spoke little and seemed unreachable and so not very available for learning through discussion and exchanges of ideas. His work was mechanical and minimal and seemed to be blocked by strong feelings which he could not express.

In one-to-one sessions, Joe avoided close involvement with the therapist and tended to divert the task to his own choices. He engaged in board games with rules and structure which was understood as his way of managing proximity, controlling interaction in the relationship and moderating his feelings. This began to change and Joe became very involved in play with the large cushions in the room. He attacked and jumped on them with savage joy and this gradually gave way to making them into a safe pathway across a dangerous swamp. It was as if his anger needed to be expressed before he could use the cushions as useful supports on his journey – as a secure base in adversity. It felt as if Joe was resolving a conflict to which he could not give words but could be acted out safely in the therapeutic context.

Joe's class teacher reported that he had become more 'available', cheerful and responsive and more interested in taking part in class activities. He talked more and his talent for making and building objects was able to be exploited in the classroom with greater success. His mother reported that he was friendlier at home. It was also as if his sense of himself and capacity to connect with others had changed.

IMPLICATIONS FOR LEARNING

LEARNING PROFILE OF PUPIL
LINKED TO AVOIDANT ATTACHMENT

Approach to school/classroom
· apparent indifference to uncertainty in new situations ·

Response to the teacher
· denial of need for support and help from the teacher ·
· sensitivity to proximity of the teacher ·

Response to the task
· need to be autonomous and independent of the teacher ·
· hostility towards the teacher is directed towards the task ·
· the task operates as an emotional safety barrier between
the pupil and the teacher ·

Skills and difficulties
· limited use of creativity ·
· likely to be underachieving ·
· limited use of language ·

Fig. 10 Learning Profile: Avoidant Attachment

From the observations of Barry and about Joe, and other similar examples, it is possible to discern a pattern of response to the teacher and to the task, which reflects the adult's specific expectation, and the child's particular involvement in the task. When a number of cases were carefully scrutinised in terms of response in the learning situation (Geddes 1999), a pattern emerged. This is presented as a Learning Profile (Figure 10) which outlines the pattern of behaviour in the learning situation, linked to the Avoidant Attachment behaviour pattern.

The Learning Triangle

The relationship dynamic within the profile can also be summarised by the Learning Triangle, in which the child avoids the relationship with the teacher, and directs his or her focus towards the task.

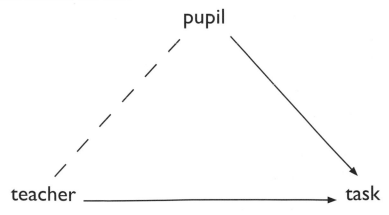

Fig. 11 Learning Triangle: Avoidant Attachment

This focus on the task indicates that it (the task) helps to moderate the experience of the relationship with the teacher, which is imbued with uncertainty about availability of acceptance and support. This behaviour can be experienced by the teacher as being ignored by the child, and it is easy to be provoked into reacting. The rejection the child experienced in its earliest relationship can be felt by the teacher. The teacher's response may be to persist in trying to help, which, unfortunately, can further trigger the Avoidant response. *"I sat him down and talked to him for an hour"* and *"he would not look at me"* are examples of how the pupil's defensive behaviour can be misunderstood.

However, the capacity to focus on the task can also be deceptive. It is possible to construe this avoidant response to the teacher as a form of independence, often welcomed in a demanding classroom. It is the *degree of avoidance* which is significant, from the severely affected experience represented by Barry's behaviour to the moderate difficulties noticed about Joe.

Intervention Implications
Avoidant Attachment

The purpose of this book is to 'make a difference' to the experience of learning for the pupil and to the experience of teaching. Over time, a catalogue of responses in terms of intervention have been experienced as well as proposed by others working in the field. The following interventions have been experienced as beneficial to pupils and to teachers in terms of learning outcomes and also increase the repertoire of educational responses which facilitated learning for children demonstrating this behavioural pattern of response in the classroom.

In relation to the teacher
- The implication for these pupils is that the teacher is imbued with negative expectations. The challenge of the task triggers uncertainties and so a need for support and proximity, which must be denied in favour of self-sufficiency. The need for help is likely to be denied and the offer

of help rejected. At the more extreme end of the continuum, anger may be triggered which is expressed towards objects and other pupils. THE RELATIONSHIP BETWEEN THE PUPIL AND THE TEACHER IS THUS MADE SAFE BY THE PRESENCE OF THE TASK, or in highly structured encounters such as games with clear rules and outcomes. This enables a closer proximity without triggering alarm and defensive reaction to the teacher.

In relation to peers

- THE PRESENCE OF ANOTHER CHILD can moderate the intensity of the teacher's proximity. This reminded me that when Barry wrote his card to his mother, exposing so much of his conflict, I was sitting next to him but actually working with another child. Pairs or small groups might help a child to experience closer proximity to the teacher but moderated by the presence of others.

- In a secondary school, Year 12 pupils worked as MENTORS with great success. In the case of a very avoidant boy, the presence of older children taking such a role enabled a discussion about his difficulties. The mentor can act as an intermediary, whose presence defuses the tensions arising from the pupil/teacher interaction, enabling the pupil about whom there is concern to contribute more to the discussion.

In relation to the task and within the curriculum

- TURNING TOWARDS THE TASK IS THE FOCUS FOR INTERVENTION. The learning task is the starting point for pupils who find relationships challenging and is also the primary arena in which the teacher's skill can be exercised. A well delivered lesson with a plan made clear at the beginning, and clear, structured tasks which can be completed with little help from the teacher with all materials to hand, can reduce the perceived threat of 'not knowing' something and feeling unsupported.

- THE NATURE OF THE TASK is also important to note. Both Barry and Joe tended to be more engaged by concrete structured activities with little use of imaginative skills. This can be enhanced by differentiation of the task which acknowledges the pupil's need to exercise some choice in terms of content and activity and to experience greater thoughtfulness of the teacher. An understanding of this pattern of response can help the pupil to experience BEING THOUGHT ABOUT AND HELD IN MIND. THIS MIRRORS EMPATHIC ATTUNEMENT, perhaps absent in infancy.

- With this group of children, verbal expression can be inhibited – perhaps a reflection of unrecognised and uncontained anxiety in infancy. Writing itself can often be associated with self-expression; such children often resist using a pen and if they do, write as if attacking the paper. Watching some children write often suggests that the pencil is a dangerous weapon! STRUCTURE can facilitate writing and help to mediate the intensity of written responses. Filling in boxes, completing sentences and writing brief sentences in defined spaces can help to calm fears about 'spilling out' onto a blank page.

- The curriculum provides many opportunities to explore hidden or dangerous feelings. Boxes, bridges, houses, castles, journeys are the basis of many stories and all have symbolic significance about closeness and distance, containment and fears. Without any conscious disclosure, many strong feelings can be given words and meaning. Emotional literacy can begin by trying to describe the experiences of characters in stories. This is also true of films, videos and even TV soaps. METAPHOR is a powerful tool when working with pupil's who are very sensitive to feelings and relationships. Such use of metaphor can help to integrate cognition and emotional function and so facilitate learning. (Davou 2003).

• STRUCTURED GAMES with rules, maths with defined procedures and clear right or wrong answers, questions which are factual and precise, sorting objects and building structures are also more likely to appeal and provide an arena for safe engagement. These concrete tasks are essentially left brain functions which help to keep strong feelings at bay and prevent flooding of the brain with intolerable emotions which can trigger reactive behaviour. The sensitivity of the teacher to the meaning of this separation of function can help to integrate cognition and emotional function and so facilitate learning rather than keep them apart to the detriment of learning (Davou 2003).

The particular significance of separation and loss

In the research sample which was investigated in relation to this pattern of early relationships and learning, other characteristics were found to be associated with Avoidant attachment patterns (Geddes 1999).

A high frequency of conduct disordered boys reflected the ongoing concern about pupil behaviour led by boys. The higher representation of absent fathers suggested that in the absence of an alternative experience of the self in relation to others, the child is more exposed to the adversity implicit in the primary attachment relationship. The findings also suggested that there was a theme of rejection, separation and loss which ran through the experiences of children who experienced this pattern of relating. Rejection reverberated with absence and unresolved loss.

It was also noted that in the sample of thirty cases investigated from inner city boroughs, most of the sample was of black and mixed race children. In a relatively small sample in inner city areas this may not have been disproportionate but the finding led to a discussion with Elaine Arnold (Arnold 1977, Separation and Reunion Forum). Links were made between the histories of Afro-Caribbean families who had experienced migration and relocation and the experience of separation and reunion which many Afro-Caribbean families had described during the years of migration in the early 1960s. From these discussions and considerations, it was concluded that recent history of disrupted attachment may continue to affect families now and be reflected in Avoidant patterns of relating. This may be a factor which contributes to the over-representation of black children in off-site education units, in the Care services and in prisons – an acting out of past experiences of separation and perceived abandonment, reverberating through the generations.

The implication of this is that the theme of endings and loss may be a crucial issue for many pupils but particularly for pupils whose families have experienced loss through relocation and migration. This sensitive area can be thought about in terms of endings in school days and terms, teachers and pupils leaving, the content of the curriculum, stories, drama, art and films. Loss is a significant experience for all pupils, but for those with a recent history of loss of family network and community, it may be particularly apposite.

Summary

- Awareness of the Avoidant pattern of behaviour and response helps us to be sensitive to the child's anxieties in the face of challenges evoked by learning, and by the close proximity of a caring and supportive figure who offers concern and assistance. The task is the barrier that defends the child against feelings of hostility, reflecting early attachment experience. Turning towards the task is the main focus of intervention.

- The teacher's understanding of the pupil's behaviour can turn the task into a bridge that links them, rather that a device which separates them. The teacher's sensitivity to the child, expressed through an understanding of the significance of the task and the need for a 'safe' proximity can help the pupil to experience himself as thought about and held in mind. This enables the development of a more positive sense of self and more hopeful expectations of others. The education experience can be a rich source of resilience to the pupil who has experienced an Avoidant early attachment.

- The overall outcome can be that the child will be able to tolerate exploration of experience and ideas with diminished anxiety. This can enhance experiences of learning and social and emotional engagement, and can assist pupils of this early Attachment experience to be more available to work (learning) and to trusting relationships.

Chapter 6

Pupils who fear separation
Resistant/Ambivalent Attachment in the classroom

Separating from the secure base, in order to explore and experience the world outside the primary relationship, is a crucial step in development. Securely attached children learn to explore with relative confidence, assured that parental support is available and reliable when they encounter distress or uncertainty. For the children who experience a less available secure base, such as the Avoidant pattern described in the previous chapter, it is sometimes necessary to adopt a false confidence and to be self-reliant in the face of uncertainty or fear. However, Ainsworth & Wittig (1969) identified a further pattern of relating, in which the child is unable to rely on the responses of the primary carer and seeks close proximity in order to guarantee some kind of certainty in the face of fear. For these children and their carers, it is separation *per se* which causes distress – the nature of Attachment experience influences the nature of the separation experience.

Children negotiate separation from their parents in a variety of ways and this is very evident when starting nursery or play group.

At the entrance to the play group, mothers entered the hall with the children, took off their coats and escorted them to the edge of the play group space. There was a gap between the front door and the beginning of the playgroup space in which this happened. It was not marked in any particular way, but it was clearly the transitional territory in which separation was negotiated. Some children made this transition themselves, and followed a direct route into the space of the playgroup. But other children had specific strategies for tackling this transisition. Over the year, I observed several regular routines.

At the edge of the transitional area and where the play space started, there was a slide in the middle, some books on one side of the room, and at the other side, a box of Brio train set and track.

Carla entered the transitional space and looked ahead of her into the play area. She slowly mounted the slide and sat at the top, poised for descent. Minutes passed and she remained at the top of the slide staring ahead. Suddenly she swooshed down, walked into the play area and engaged with a worker at the table where an activity was laid out.

Brandon left his mother, looking very sad as he glanced back at her in the doorway holding the new baby. As usual, he walked slowly across the space and sank down at the Brio box. He set out the track, joining up the parts into a continuous circle. He joined up the train and pushed it around, made one or two circuits of the track; then stood up, and entered the play area. There he sat on a bicycle for a while, and then entered the activity area.

Jordan dashed across the space and into the play area. He went straight to the home corner and began to put himself to bed. He then drank from the baby bottle and then got up, 'got dressed' and joined in the activities, as if re-enacting the routine of getting up and leaving home.

Janet walked slowly in and without looking behind, walked to the books. She picked a book, sank to the floor and looked at the pictures for a long time. She then joined the activities.

These routines and rituals appeared to be linked to the separation from home which took place at the doorway. In various ways, they represented something about the experience of separation for each child, and how it could be negotiated. The experience is located at an earlier stage, when the infant first experiences the 'me' and 'not me'. When playing 'peek a boo' and 'hide and seek' and 'find me', the infant is exploring the separation which must inevitably occur, in order to experience the self as separate (and 'me') and to explore the wider world. This process is also an outcome of the mother's capacities to let go of the infant, to experience herself as separate from her baby and to tolerate her own separation and autonomy.

> How selfhood begins with walking away
> And love is proved in the letting go   (C.S. Lewis)

For some mothers this can be a challenge, affecting the Attachment relationship, and having implications for the child's engagement in learning.

Pupils who fail to make a successful engagement at school and who have high absence rates are very likely to underachieve, and are prone to limited engagement in society as adults. The characteristics of attachment behaviour of children described in this chapter tend to fall into this category of vulnerability. Their behaviour pattern is dominated by *separation anxiety,* which can be apparent from their earliest attendance. Behaviour associated with this early experience will be presented and discussed here, as in the previous chapter; from identification of characteristics of the pattern noted in the Strange Situation Procedure, through how it might be experienced by the child, to what behaviour might be associated with learning, to proposals for intervention in school.

CHARACTERISTICS OF RESISTANT/AMBIVALENT ATTACHMENT BEHAVIOUR

Within the original sample researched by Ainsworth & Wittig (1969), (in the Strange Situation Procedure) a group of children was identified who were anxious in their mother's presence and were very upset when separated from her. At reunion they wanted contact but resisted it, as if finding 'little security in the mother's return or presence' (Main & Weston 1982, p.39) and demonstrating an ambivalence towards her. The behaviour of the mothers of these babies was diverse but they were not rejecting. They were highly insensitive to the infant's experience but seemed to enjoy bodily contact, perhaps more in response to their own needs that those of the baby. Clinical observation suggests that some mothers may have overwhelming and unresolved needs of their own. These needs may take precedence over the needs of their children. The mother's needs are being met in the relationship with the child and take priority over the needs of the child. This parental trait could be described as intrusive or enmeshed (Barrett & Trevitt 1991).

HOW THE CHILD MIGHT FEEL

Ainsworth writes, 'The conflict of the ... babies is a simple one – between wanting close bodily contact and angry because their mothers do not pick them up when they want to be held or hold them for as long as they want. Because their mothers are insensitive to their signals, (the) babies lack confidence in their (mother's) responsiveness. Thus when the attachment system is highly activated, (these) babies are doubly upset because they have learned to expect to be frustrated rather than comforted' (Ainsworth 1982, p.18).

Hopkins (1990) uses Balint's (1959) description of similar behaviour, and quotes; the 'real aim (of the infant) is not to cling but to be held without even needing to express the wish for it' and 'physical contact is necessary in order to keep 'in touch' (p.22).

Clinging may be the attachment behaviour aimed at holding the mother close. In the light of Bowlby's comments about 'fear' (1973, p.107), the infants may be responding to fear of the absence of the loved one, by making sure they do not go away. Erickson et al (1985) described such children as having two distinct types of response in the pre-school situation. They can be either impulsive and tense, or helpless and fearful. In terms of anger, Sroufe (1983) observed that the resistant infants directed their anger at the mother.

The attachment behaviour of these children is organised around an attachment figure who finds separation difficult, whose own needs tend to lead the relationship in such a way that there is little sensitivity to the separate and differing needs of the child. In the research sample that was investigated (Geddes 1999) such a carer tended to have very weak boundaries and little parental control, as if not confident of their own adult authority. They described their significant life events as accidents, illnesses, injuries – a tendency to somatise (physically experience) rather than endure emotional distress and perhaps, as Holmes would say, to experience *'the hospital as the surrogate secure base'* (Holmes 2001, p.29). With a high level of separation anxiety the children of this attachment relationship are often identified by poor school attendance and they can be particularly vulnerable at transition to secondary school.

From the perspective of the children, they experience the attachment relationship as one in which separation and autonomy are denied in favour of anxious involvement with the primary carer. Attachment behaviour is dominated by uncertainty that their attachment needs will be met, and by ambivalence expressed as both clinging and controlling behaviour. It is as if they have had to focus closely on the parental state of mind to optimise their chances of getting a response (Gerhardt 2004). They can also be overtly hostile, and mothers will often complain that they have been hit and attacked by their own child .

Individual work with children of different ages is described here to demonstrate the nature of their struggle to learn, and also to demonstrate how children can change through the educational process.

Examples from practice

Work with Len.

Len was a well-built seven year old, who had been excluded from school because of aggressive behaviour towards the teacher. He seemed relaxed and comfortable in the one-to-one teaching situation with the Home Tutor who visited him in his home. It was as if he was welcoming a guest. But gradually his pleasant gentlemanly manner gave way to commands and attempts to take over, as the tutor persisted in setting a task. If the tutor planned to begin with English, Len would suggest that it should be maths. If a maths task was introduced, he would complain that the tutor had promised to start with drawings. It was some time before it was possible to distinguish who was the teacher and who was the pupil. Len's first squiggle picture seemed to depict his inner struggle.

*His squiggle put himself firmly inside my circle and another mark was transformed into the word **'me'** written clearly inside my circle. He wrote that it was about **'me and mo'** who seem to become muddled up into the same word – **'omeeo'**. It seemed a clear depiction of his undifferentiated state and hinted at the anxious feelings that the requirements of independent thoughts and learning might involve.*

In the accompanying text he wrote; 'One day me and mo were looking at each other and he ate her up, he did not like her. Because

Fig. 12 Len's drawing

she bossed him around'.

   Len's energy seemed directed at controlling the tutor as if he could not tolerate me having an idea that was not his idea. The task was an irrelevant intrusion, threatening to separate him from me. Holding onto the role as the teacher was difficult and involved tolerating a great deal of resistance and hostility. Len seemed to need to behave in this way so that he could experience us as separate.

   With persistence, Len began to experience the task as an action outside the primary relationship – the world outside **'me and mo'.** *In his drawings and stories, other objects and people began to appear. His figures acquired wheels and travelled along roads with bridges, suggesting an exploration* *of separation and change. He could experience a sense of agency in having ideas of his own. After the final session he suggested a walk along the riverbank outside his house, as if the outside world could now be experienced with some interest and excitement. I later met Len when he was awaiting a new school place, and he said he was looking forward to going to school again.*

In this relationship, it seemed to be the teacher's role to contain Len's anxieties as he experienced the world outside '*me and mo*', and so the future possibilities of the outside world. The role of the teacher seemed to represent the presence of an independent 'significant other'; as someone who could believe in Len's capacity to experience himself as separate and to engage in the task, and by implication, in the future with the outside world. The task seemed to become a symbolic presence acting as a bridge to learning about the outside world.

The second example shows how a teenage girl was able to work through the metaphor of the educational task of story writing, and thus make her own journey towards autonomy, to experiencing herself differently and to having her own thoughts.

Work with Naomi

Naomi was twelve and had never attended secondary school. She was described as school phobic. She remained at home with her mother. She did not go out alone. After a few sessions at home, further sessions were offered at a local family centre where Naomi was escorted in a taxi. It took some time for mother and Naomi to adapt to this arrangement. Mother was concerned about 'something happening' on the way to the centre.

In this separate space, and within a one-to-one relationship, Naomi soon became engaged in learning tasks. At first, these tasks closely followed the school curriculum in various subjects, and it seemed as if Naomi was trying to be a model pupil. After a short time, she discovered story writing and she wrote prolifically. These stories demonstrate her separation and individuation journey very eloquently.

The character in one story finds a box, in which a secret about her identity has been hidden as if the parents had not told her who she was. She begins to explore her new identity. A magic process begins which takes her to a strange place, a planet where they do not communicate by speaking but by understanding each other's thoughts. (I wondered about the room where we met and her experience of the shared but separate thinking about her story). Eventually, she is reunited with her true family; for a while, she feels confused by her new identity, and so returns to Earth for a visit to her old family. But as time goes by, she becomes accustomed to who she really is, and decides to stay on the Planet and visit her Earth parents occasionally – clear about who she now is and separate from them.

There are a multitude of meanings in this story, but it seemed that Naomi was exploring separation and could now contemplate the journey from home assured of a safe return.

Naomi next chose to write about a refugee girl who has to make a journey alone back to her own country. The boat she is on sinks and she is washed up on an island. She is cared for by the tribe that lives there and she makes a friend. The friend helps her to overcome her fear of the sea and teaches her how to swim. In return, the girl finds that she can design interesting hair styles and jewellery, and soon she is accepted as a member of the tribe with skills that are valued. Naomi writes that 'She feels important and valued and realises how happy she is'.

Naomi may have been describing the experience of negotiating the gap between home and the family centre, where the teacher helped her to find skills and a mind of her own. She had begun to find the task/ world interesting and rewarding. She ended the story with a letter to her mum and dad saying that she was safe and happy and wasn't coming home. This seemed Naomi's separation obituary. She had survived the shipwreck of separation with the help of a 'friend'. She experienced her difference as new and interesting. Naomi continued to write and to explore her own history in the metaphor of stories. Naomi did not take up a school place, but a year later contacted me for a reference to attend a course at a further education college.

Journey stories remain an important tool in work with pupils who are negotiating separation, autonomy and new ways of relating (Morton 2004, Waters 2004).

In different settings the work can take place to include the parent. This can be a sensitive area to work in. The parent's unrecognised and unmet needs can block thinking about the child.

Colin lived with his mother and father. He refused to go to his new secondary school and at home, his mother was upset by his aggression and rudeness to her. However she acknowledged that they had a special relationship. During the day, Colin helped his mother in her child-minding job at home, and in the evenings, she and Colin sat in one room watching soaps on TV whilst Colin's dad sat in another room watching 'his' programmes – sport and news programmes. The split seemed clear, between preoccupations with relationships and engagement in the outside world. Colin's mother was persuaded to let Colin's father support her in putting pressure on Colin to go to school. The strengthened collaboration between mother and father appeared to release Colin and within a week he was attending a support unit as a transitional step before going back to school.

In a sweep on non-attenders in the London Borough of Islington, The Guardian summarised the findings by the comment, 'Often parents just want company when they go shopping' (Guardian 2002). For some mothers, the fear of their own isolation is intolerable. Often this may involve depression, or unresolved fears from the past, about which they cannot bear to think. For some children, the need to 'take care of' their vulnerable parent can proccupy them and intrude into school attendance.

In the research sample investigated in relation to responses in the learning situation (Geddes 1999), the children with this pattern of behaviour were very anxious, and tended to cling to the teacher. They tried to take over her role, ignoring the task, as if it was an intrusion into the space between them. The children commonly demonstrated good verbal skills which could be used to dominate and manipulate the teacher's attention. Their educational achievement was often poor as if attention to the task distracted them from the need to be attuned to the teacher. They could also be hostile towards the teacher if their wishes were not met. Teachers often describe them as dependent, but it may be more useful to think of these children as anxiously controlling, expressing a fear of loss of adult attention and presence.

For children whose experience has been of a Resistant/Ambivalent attachment pattern, responses in the classroom towards the teacher and the task are likely to reflect certain characteristics.

IMPLICATIONS FOR LEARNING

LEARNING PROFILE OF PUPIL
LINKED TO RESISTANT/AMBIVALENT
ATTACHMENT

**Approach to the school
and the classroom**
· high level of anxiety and uncertainty ·

Response to the teacher
· need to hold onto the attention of the teacher ·
· apparent dependence on the teacher in
order to engage in learning ·
· expressed hostility towards the teacher when frustrated ·

Response to the task
· difficulties attempting the task if unsupported ·
· unable to focus on the task for fear
of losing teacher's attention ·

Skills and Difficulties
· likely to be underachieving ·
· language may be well developed but not
consistent with levels of achievement ·
· numeracy may be weak ·

Fig. 13 LearningProfile: Resistant/Ambivalent Attachment

Learning Triangle

The Learning Triangle for this pattern reflects the tension between the pupil and adult at the expense of the task; interpreted in terms of early relationships, it may demonstrate an unresolved conflict which does not permit 'another' to intrude into the mother/child dyad. Beaumont (1989) quotes from Britten et al (1989), who comments that until the child can tolerate the position of being a witness of his or her parent's relationship, and not a participant he or she is going to remain inextricably merged with his mother. In the learning situation, the child is preoccupied with the relationship with the teacher, at the expense of the task.

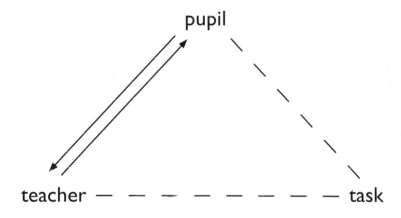

Fig. 14 Learning Triangle: Resistant/Ambivalent Attachment

Intervention Implications
Resistant/Ambivalent

The implications for children in the Resistant/Ambivalent Attachment group is that the first step they need to take is to engage with the task, in order to begin the process of change. For the teacher, recognising the pupil's separation anxiety helps to give the behaviour meaning and to inform practice. The pupil can be experienced as dependent and often irritating and intrusive. It can help those engaged in individual support of such children to be aware of the child's powerful wish to achieve a merged state with the adult by seeming to need a very high level of support; and to recognise the fear and anger the child experiences when adult attention is not under their control. It may be more helpful to reframe this behaviour as an anxious dependence and a need to control the significant adult who has not been experienced as reliably present. It is important that the adult remains the adult in charge and neither replicate the neediness of the primary carer, nor collude with the child's apparent pseudo-adult helper role.

In the task and within the curriculum

- DIFFERENTIATION OF THE TASK into small independent steps, and TURN-TAKING, to model the experience of two separate people working alongside each other, rather than merging with each other.
- A TIMER can help moderate anxiety during short, timed, independent tasks.
- BOARD GAMES provide separation and can also create opportunities to express hostility towards adults in a safe manner – with structure and rules.
- HOLDING A SPECIAL (TRANSITIONAL) OBJECT can take the place of the teacher for short periods – *"please look after this for me for a while"*.
- MAKING EXPLICIT COMMENTS across the classroom can be reassuring. They demonstrate that the teacher is aware of the pupil and thinking about him or her.
- THE CURRICULUM and stories in particular, can provide a rich source of material to facilitate thinking and emotional development around issues of separation, identity and independence.

In relation to peers

- Children who have experienced a closely enmeshed relationship with their carer, and whose impulse may be to take charge of the carer in order to maintain and predict their attention and presence, may have become very sensitive to the state of mind of the carer. They may develop a capacity to be tuned into others in a way that will enable them to predict and control others in order to re-assure themselves. This can be experienced by others as very bossy and controlling; girls in particular can become very unpopular. For some children this capacity can become an asset in the classroom when appropriately directed into being helpful to the class in ways other than caring for others -- RESPONSIBILITY FOR TASKS, RATHER THAN PEOPLE. The children can then experience themselves as involved with others as well as functioning with some degree of independence.

- SMALL GROUP WORK which facilitates peer relationships and provides opportunities to explore experience through stories of imaginary journeys enables the child to experience anxiety safely, find support from peers and experience having a 'mind of their own'. (Morton 2000, Waters 2004)

In the planning

- PLANNING BEGINNINGS, SEPARATIONS AND ENDINGS can help the transition into school and at the end of the day. Sometimes the anxiety may be eased by a planned withdrawal of the parent, or a brief time in the office before going into class. The space in which the transition is negotiated may help to diminish anxiety. In the Early Years, the opportunity to engage in creative play can facilitate transition and relieve separation anxiety as in the examples given at the beginning of this chapter.

- PLANNING AND WARNINGS OF CHANGES AND CLASS MOVEMENTS can ease separation anxiety being triggered when changes take place. Particular preparation will be needed for the transition to secondary school.

- Regular absence from school is often an indicator of the resistant/ ambivalent experience, and PROCEDURES WHICH RESPOND QUICKLY TO ABSENCE help the child to feel held in mind appropriately by the school. This will lead to an experience of the reliability of the school system.

In relation to the teacher

- A prime characteristic of responsiveness to this pattern of relating is RELIABLE AND CONSISTENT ADULT SUPPORT which does not collude with dependency. The presence of a specific person to 'go to' on arrival in nursery can assuage separation anxiety. In a study of a nursery school with a high intake of vulnerable children, Barnet & Bain (1986), found that in the presence of a consistent adult figure to whom the child could relate, stress levels in the child did not rise and development was enhanced. This has implications for management of staff and duty rotas so that staff can be consistent. This can also be relevant to pupils in transition to secondary school where it can be helpful to identify one named contact person, perhaps a mentor, who can meet the child each morning and assist in the relatively complex changes of classes and teachers in a secondary school day.

- Within a family context, a further implication of this attachment pattern in relation to the school child relates to non-attendance and school phobia. Many children are absent with parental collusion. The pattern of behaviour associated with this attachment experience suggests that separation anxiety is the tension that fuels absence and that this may arise from within the mother but be expressed by the child. Material from research data (Geddes 1999) suggests that illness, accidents and injury are frequently associated with this pattern. This does not deny the reality of illness, but suggests that physical ailments can be associated with separation anxiety with which parents may collude. A further useful intervention therefore may be to INVOLVE THE PARENT/S. The mother/father relationship has sometimes seemed blurred in favour of the mother/child relationship, as in the example of Colin (p.94). A strengthened alliance between the parents, or an alliance with the teacher and the parent, may help to divert the parental need for merging with the child into a more adult and appropriate relationship, thus ENGAGING THE PARENT'S POTENTIAL TO CHANGE.

- Other services are often involved, Education Welfare Officers in particular. Involvement of the Child and Adolescent Mental Health Service may also be helpful and CONTACT WITHIN NETWORKS can strengthen the framework around consistent expectations and planning.

- The recent discussions of fines and imprisonment of parent/s for non-attendance at school does little to relieve the situation. Perhaps instead of forced absence of the parent with implications for the whole family, it would be more helpful to FACILITATE SEPARATION OF THE CHILD BY ATTENDANCE AT DAILY EDUCATIONAL SESSIONS IN A SMALL SETTING. Here gradual engagement in the learning task, with a high level of support and association with a small group of others, could facilitate separation and the autonomous identity of the child.

Summary

- The vulnerability for these pupils lies in the challenges of separation and the fear of being 'lost from mind', which triggers an intense response to cling, to possess and to intrude. School attendance can be a challenge, as can be the 'intrusion' represented by the educational task. At transition to secondary school this issue will be highlighted: for some, it will represent overwhelming anxiety. The relative safety of the primary classroom with the same teacher is challenged by the necessity to engage with a number of teachers and lesson changes in the secondary school. Children in the Resistant/Ambivalent group can feel particularly vulnerable when the parent's needs continue to overwhelm the relationship and other agencies may then be needed to intervene at a family level. Inability to attend secondary school can thus lead to significant social exclusion with implications for cycles of disadvantage in future generations.

- However, these children can thrive in schools where reliable and consistent adults can stand in for the parent as alternative 'attachment figures'. Such adults enhance the child's potential to separate and through engagement in the task, experience themselves as autonomous and with a mind of their own. Finding a capacity to be involved in the task implies the possibility of future involvement in society, and a break in the pattern of family behaviour.

Chapter 7

The most worrying pupils
Disorganised/Disorientated Attachment in the classroom

Jim was having a typically hard day. He sat at the table in the Year 4 classroom, with a fixed and furious gaze. He muttered when the teacher spoke, and then stood up and moved around restlessly as the teacher continued to deliver the lesson to the class. When asked to return to his seat, he dragged the chair out noisily and banged it in again. He continued to distract other children near him but the teacher managed to maintain the class' attention and focus. When asked directly to turn to the task, Jim swept the sheet off the table; muttering loudly and offensively, he stormed out of the room, banging the door. He walked purposefully along the corridor, ignoring enquiries, entreaties and instruction to return to class and get on with learning. He walked out of the door and onto the playing field where he charged about unresponsive to requests or instructions to return.

The regular and persistent violation of all the classroom expectations had the teacher exhausted and distressed. Jim's mother was regularly invited to discuss Jim's progress but more often than not did not keep the arrangements. It was as if she wanted to make a difference but could not face really thinking about his difficulties or feelings.

Jim is an example of a small but significant group of children whose presence in school is accompanied by severe and challenging behaviour which tests all the practices that services can offer. It often involves exclusions, both temporary and permanent. Very often engagement with parent/s is difficult, and the school can feel embattled with an intractable 'problem child'. Policies of inclusion can feel persecutory to the school. The situation can become a postponement of an almost inevitable crisis at transition to secondary school, when the pupil meets the different challenges of the larger and more demanding institution. The cycle of crisis and failed intervention can continue.

This small minority of very challenging pupils can be identified very readily and it is easy to predict a difficult future for a child who has such little capacity to engage in the social and learning opportunities of school. Behaviour such as Jim's may represent an early experience of highly adverse attachment known as Disorganised Attachment. As in previous chapters, this behaviour pattern will be presented and discussed in terms of the research findings which identified the pattern. I will go on to consider what the experience of the child might be, relate this to examples from practice and present a profile of possible behaviour in school. Interventions will also be proposed and discussed, related to attachment experience.

Characteristics of the Disorganised Attachment pattern

In the original Strange Situation research sample, a small number of cases were identified which demonstrated an inconsistent pattern of attachment behaviour (Main & Solomon 1982). It was a difficult pattern to identify precisely as it was found in conjunction with behaviour patterns characteristic of one or other of the categories of attachment behaviour described previously. Whereas the Avoidant or Ambivalent infants have developed consistent patterns of response, these infants did not appear to have consistent strategies for dealing with stress (hence the term Disorganised/

Disorientated). Typical disorientated behaviour in the Strange Situation was:

- proximity seeking followed by avoidance
- contradictory behaviour patterns such as approaching with head averted or looking away whilst being held
- undirected displays of anxiety such as rocking
- direct expressions of confusion or apprehension such as hand in mouth gestures when mother returns to the room
- behavioural stilling, when all movements cease, suggesting confusion or depression: and dazed expressions suggestive of conflicting systems producing a frozen state.

Implications for the feelings and behaviour of the child

For children of this pattern, early relationships may have been dominated by the overwhelming preoccupations and high levels of stress and distress in the primary carer, with implications for neglect of the child or possibly actual harm. Such a parent may have been frightening to the child. Some parents may have been emotionally, physically or sexually abusive. Others may have been suffering from unresolved grief and mourning, and others from drug related problems resulting in periods of major pre-occupation or emotional absence. The child may have been exposed to continuous marital strife and violence. There may also have been experiences of abandonment without a consistent replacement carer, (for example, the children experiencing the extreme neglect of the Romanian orphanages) or frequent changes of carer with little continuity of thought and feelings.

These antecedents of distress and anxiety have implications for the basic experience the child needs most, a sense of safety in the face of emotional or physical threat. It is important to recall however, that the threat is not always of actual harm but may be harm by default; such as the emotional abandonment that children can experience when a parent is present, but absent and unavailable because of alcohol or drug misuse or because of mental illness. Carers of such children may be difficult to contact because of their own history of insecurity, and they too may be sensitive to thinking about their own painful experiences which are perpetuated by being acted out through their children. Clearly the implications for emotional development are considerable.

In such situations, children are likely to have experienced absence of responsiveness and care as well as threat from the source of their security. Fairbairn (1952) describes this situation as like being starving but faced with a 'poisoned cake'. Hopkins (1990) observes that: 'As these infants grow up they are liable to cope with their helplessness by becoming very controlling of their parents, either in a care-giving or a punitive way'. Mary Sue Moore (1995) supports this view and describes this as a pattern of behaviour organized around uncertainty and threat and involving a need for considerable hyper-vigilance in the face of uncontained anxiety and fears.

In the absence of a secure base such children may grow up with constant and overwhelming fears, anxiety and helplessness. They may have to be on constant alert for immediate danger – hyper-vigilant. The brain is 'use-dependent'; in the earliest years, the right hemisphere of the brain is developing, and responsive to stimulation from the environment. In the absence of a secure emotional base, the infant is left in a high state of arousal with little capacity for self-regulation (Schore 1994). Brain development may then become dominated by reactivity to danger with reinforced pathways for fight and flight which are easily triggered (discussed more fully in Chapter 3).

Mary Sue Moore (Caspari Foundation Lecture March 2005) described the response of a refugee child to a sudden noise.

He dropped to the floor and under the table. It was as if the pathway for flight had been triggered in an instant and his response was dominated by procedural memory of past experiences of terror not under his conscious control.

The nature of this behaviour, experienced as irrational, without any apparent meaning, cannot be 'explained' and is very baffling in the classroom. There appears to be no way of understanding or communicating about it.

The behaviour of children who experience such overwhelming and uncontained anxiety is clearly affected and organised around survival and defending against overwhelming fear and uncertainty. This has profound implications for learning. Behaviour is likely to reflect key experiences.

- In the absence of a person who can consistently think about the child with sensitivity to his or her experiences, an impaired process of relatedness and reflectiveness can result, with little capacity for self-awareness and sensitivity to others – a lack of empathy.

- In the absence of continuity of care, a sense of time and continuity of narrative may be impaired (Bain & Barnet 1980) affecting memory. Experience may seem disjointed and learning becomes a series of events rather than coherent and integrated knowledge.

- Such children may be very sensitive to the denigration they experience, in perceiving themselves as unworthy of anyone's care; they may show this as sensitivity to any form of perceived disrespect. Their Internal Working Model (see p.43) of themselves may be of an undeserving child of little value. Their expectation of the world may be of danger, hostility and disregard. With little experience of support in the face of challenge and adversity, anything that they do not know or understand may be perceived as a threat and a humiliation.

- Comments on the origins of anger also link this experience of early emotional adversity with strong feelings of rage. The APA Commission on Violence (1993) link aggression and violence to weak bonding in infancy and weak parenting. Harlow's apes (1974), brought up in the absence of parental care, physically attacked their offspring. De Zulueta (1993) comments that 'violent behaviour is an intrinsic aspect of the clinical picture' for sexually abused children (p.194). Kohut (1972) writes about the need that 'calls forth rage to protect the self from feelings of infantile vulnerability' (in Fonagy 2001, p.110). Holmes (2001) also describes outbursts of rage as a 'form of displacement activity' (p.13) triggered when an individual is torn between fear and need.

From such comments it is clear that children with this early experience are likely to be identified by high levels of reactivity to stress, and expressions of rage, anger and aggression.

Responses to school and to learning

In an early educational therapy session with Jim, he ignored the task that I had set, as usual, and rhythmically threw a sponge ball against the wall, catching it skilfully. He said it must not touch the ground or it would explode. When I introduced a conversation he talked over me as if he could not bear to let me talk. As he rhythmically threw and caught the ball, he began to talk about how he entered his own world when he was worried and that he thought he had done that when he was about three when he had been very frightened.

In the frightening 'absences' of his mother's severe pre-occupations, Jim had developed his own strategy for survival – escape into his own world where he could control what happened. His determination to be in control at whatever cost was causing his difficulties in class.

Disorganised behaviour represents a failure to integrate feelings and thoughts with profound implications for learning. Development of right brain reactivity dominates over left brain thinking function (Schore 1994). The pupil in school with such an experience of relationships and sense of self is likely to:

- appear in a heightened state of anxiety
- be highly vigilant and notice any slight distraction
- have an absence of trust in the authority of adults
- be insensitive to others' feelings
- place considerable importance on objects rather than relationships
- may bully others perceived as vulnerable/reminders of their own vulnerability
- get into trouble a lot in relatively unsupervised settings such as the playground
- experience overwhelming affect (feeling) which has no apparent meaning
- suddenly react to unseen triggers
- be extremely sensitive to criticism and implied humiliation
- have little development of the capacity to reflect
- may experience separation, fostering and Care services

– and sadly, to appear to enjoy very little.

It should be noted here that this pattern of reactive behaviour can easily be confused with ADHD and many children may become medicated for ADHD when they may actually be demonstrating a Disorganised/Disorientated attachment pattern (sometimes known as Reactive Attachment Disorder). It is important to distinguish these conditions, as prescription of medication may disguise needs that can be met in different ways which address the source of the difficulty rather than the symptoms alone. This is a contentious area, and highlights the importance of collaboration between agencies about very worrying pupil behaviour.

Examples from practice

Coral lived with foster carers. She was a diminutive five year old, and was close to exclusion. She entered the room, dashing in on tip toes and running in circuits around the furniture, sweeping objects from the cupboards onto the floor. Efforts to call her to the table, engage her in the task laid out there, hold her to prevent further disasters were met with spitting, kicking and screaming. She could not be engaged with direct attention and eventually she was left to spin and circle about until the other children in the small group had settled and were all on task. After this behaviour had been ignored for a while by the staff, Coral approached the table and sat in the vacant chair. The task was nudged in front of her. It was to join the dots forming her name. This became a starting point. The task of name writing was developed from shadow writing, to copying her name; then drawing round big plastic letters, colouring them in, then finally cutting them out and putting them in the correct order. It became a starting ritual to assemble the jumble of letters into a coherent order which was her name. She seemed able to begin the class when a concrete procedure (which identified who she was) was accomplished.

As the structure of the group became clear Coral began to imitate the others. She appeared to be able to conform to the structure and expectations of the group by observing and copying the others rather than by accepting the adult's instructions. It was as if she could conform by adaptation rather than by engaging in relationships. When she wanted the teacher to read her a story she pushed herself onto the chair the teacher was already sitting on. She picked up the reading book and pushed it into the space between her face and the teacher's. She began to make crude indications that she wanted the teacher to do something with her exclusively. It was as if she had little perception of how to share an experience between two persons.

The hopeful characteristic about Coral was that she seemed to want something from the adult. She particularly liked to have stories read to her exclusively. It felt as if she wanted to share an understanding about something with an adult, perhaps seeking a possible understanding of the narrative of her own story/experiences – a before, middle and after. She gradually accommodated to the expectations of the sessions. Over time, she became able to more or less accept instruction, follow the rules and take part in learning activities. A significant experience arose from the story 'Charlie's House' (Schermbrucker & Daly) followed by the activity of constructing a small house in a shoe box. This was a very precious item to Coral. She seemed to be constructing a physical container which paralleled her experience of finding some containment. Coral was moved to new foster parents and to a new school where she was reported to be making some progress.

△ △ △ △ △ △ △ △

Lewis was five and in the same group and his initial responses were somewhat the same. He was highly reactive to any stimulus and very difficult to engage. He had the added disadvantage of having experienced considerable and traumatising violence. His first responsive involvement was also a desire to have a story read to him exclusively by the teacher. The story chosen was from a series of early readers and called 'Monster goes to the City' (Blance & Cook) in which the lonely monster seeks a house to live in. Monster finds the perfect house that fits his awkward shape. Like Coral, Lewis seemed to be seeking an image of a physical container through stories and pictures. He made his first story book based on this theme in which he drew Monster's house; this was the starting point of his struggle to learn.

Lewis' attempts to learn, however, always seemed imbued with catastrophic expectations of failure. He could not bear to see the other pupils reading or succeeding in tasks which he could not attempt himself. He continued to strive to control the teachers and evade the pain and humiliation of not knowing. He could sequence numbers up to ten and engage with a story in which he identified with the content, but attempting any new task which he could not already do seemed an unbearable experience triggering further reactive behaviour.

Over time a series of stories seemed to make sense to him. In the Oxford Reading Tree series a family chooses a dog at the dogs' home. Lewis' first read word was 'dog' and he attempted to read the brief series of stories about Floppy the dog in which Floppy is misunderstood and blamed for something bad, and is then understood and becomes a hero. Finding a place to live and being accepted, understood and then appreciated seemed to be at the core of the metaphor.

Sometime later, in the mainstream classroom situation, one year below his chronological age and with a high level of individual support, Lewis showed similar characteristics to Coral in being able to imitate the other pupils and conform to the expectations of the classroom structures and rituals. Providing he was not told directly what to do by the teacher, he would obey the class rules. If directly instructed to sit on the carpet he would jump up and begin to run about in mindless activity. But if the teacher said that everybody in the room was expected to sit on the carpet he would comply. Imitation seemed a way of adapting rather than obeying adult instruction. With a high level of support he could begin to attempt the tasks that others in class were doing. His concentration span was very short, but he could engage in brief paper tasks if they were interspersed with mechanical tasks on the computer. It seemed possible that he might begin to learn when safe in a predictable and relatively unchallenging routine with adequate support.

After a series of fostering breakdowns, Lewis was moved to a children's home and ultimately a place was found for him in a special day school nearby. Lewis began to learn and read competently. The combination of consistent care in a structured setting in close collaboration with his school was probably at the core of his apparent progress.

When children have had the problematic experiences described in this chapter when they are very young, their behaviour towards the teacher and the learning task may be highly affected. From a series of cases in educational and clinical settings, the following profile has been constructed which links attachment experience and behaviour to learning.

IMPLICATIONS FOR LEARNING

LEARNING PROFILE OF
PUPIL LINKED TO
DISORGANISED/DISORIENTATED
ATTACHMENT

Approach to school/classroom

· intense anxiety which may be expressed as
controlling and omnipotent ·

Response to the teacher

· great difficulty experiencing trust in the authority of the
teacher but may submit to the authority of the head of the school ·
· may be unable to accept being taught, and/or unable to 'permit' the
teacher to know more than they do ·

Response to the task

· the task may seem like a challenge to their fears of incompetence,
triggering overwhelming feelings of humiliation and rejection of the task ·
· difficulty accepting 'not knowing' ·
· may appear omnipotent and to know everything already ·

Skills and difficulties

· may seem unimaginative and uncreative, and find
conceptual thought difficult ·
· likely to be underachieving and possibly
at a very immature stage of learning ·

Fig. 15 Learning Profile: Disorganised/Disorientated Attachment

The accompanying Learning Triangle for this behaviour pattern summarises the difficulties in learning when both relationships and the task are perceived as threatening: the relationship with the teacher is contaminated by the unreliability of the original attachment figure, and the task threatens a very fragile sense of self competence.

Learning Triangle associated with Disorganised/Disorientated attachment behaviour

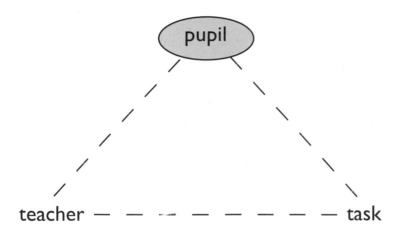

Fig. 16 Learning Triangle: Disorganised/Disorientated Attachment

This triangular model demonstrates the difficulties in engaging with the teacher and with the learning task and has long term implications for future adult relationships and access in society. The fear of many who work with these children is that there may be long term implications for mental health and offending.

Intervention Implications
Disorganised/Disorientated

Such an extreme experience of fear demonstrated in this attachment pattern suggests that these children are highly vulnerable; and Winnicott suggested that the physical containment of 'a prison cell' is a likely outcome for children who have not been psychologically held. The behaviour and responses of Coral, Lewis and Jim suggest that there is a need to experience sufficient containment, both physical and emotional, before any thinking can be possible. Developing a system within schools which can meet these needs can be a challenge. Classroom experience, post-adoption work (Hughes 1997) and contributions by colleagues can perhaps inform us about reducing anxiety levels, so that a process of change can begin.

Characteristics of interventions which may have contributed to more hopeful behaviour are discussed here as possible factors which increase the resilience potential for children and young people who have experienced extreme social and emotional adversity. This would include Looked After children who have experienced traumatic loss of their primary attachment figure, and possibly multiple changes of carer.

• Early identification

From experience of pupils with such difficulties across the age range, it seems evident that this pattern of behaviour can be identified at a very early age. The longer that children experience life with such limited emotional and physical containment, the more difficult it becomes to change the reactive pattern of behaviour which develops as a defence against extreme anxiety. Given the clear characteristics that are evident and the level of vulnerability that is implied, early intervention is essential and it may be possible to regard these pupils as 'highly vulnerable to educational and social disadvantage' or 'developmental vulnerability' to which there needs to be an immediate intervention plan with appropriate resources available. The cost in later life is far higher if such needs identified in early years are not recognised and resourced.

• Reliable and predictable routine

From the examples described, a response in the context of a relationship is not necessarily the most immediate need. 'Love' may not be enough. The level of risk and absence of safety implied in the behaviour pattern suggests that the priority is safety, reliability and predictability. The first experience of this may be to attend a place on a regular basis; the school, the unit, the building, in which safety is assured and actively promoted by rules which focus on keeping people and things safe. School may be the first experience of a structured day with predictable activities and rituals. Reliable rules and practices help to regulate brain pathways (Gerhardt 2004). Perhaps understandably, these children are often 'persistent attenders' and not prone to erratic attendance.

A reliable regime offers the child the opportunity to use their skills of adaptation to conform to an environment. This can reduce his or her high level of anxiety which drives the need for hyper-vigilance to risk and danger, and thus can minimise reactivity.

• A physical container

The experience of physical containment may be a necessary precursor to the experience of emotional containment. The concrete, physical nature of the object of safety, the house, the box, may be the first symbolic experience of a 'secure base', a necessary precursor from which to explore, find interest in the world and to learn. The closure of residential schools, which offered full time care and residency to very needy and vulnerable children, may well be a loss for those who need to experience a very high level of physical containment for long enough to then be able to look towards relationships as a source of emotional containment.

Kalu describes an experience, similar to that of Coral and Lewis, of a child finding a physical container from which to begin to learn.

> *Alex quietly made himself a 'house' about a metre square, and sat in it with the door shut ... It was the first thing I recall him being pleased with. He neither rubbished it nor destroyed it. ... the 'kennel' became the focus of his individual lessons. Inside he would read to me ... he began to talk to me from the safety of the inside about the bullying he received at home from his brother, his worries about his mum and his fears for himself ... He became more able to look at some of his worries instead of constantly being a prey to an anxious chaos ... It was a beginning again for Alex who slowly began to learn.* (Kalu 2003)

△ △ △ △ △ △ △ △

A small group of four or five girls in Years 7 to 9 were persistent attenders at their school but spent their time together wandering out of class and around the corridors, causing minor disruptions and not attending lessons. They sometimes left the school, but were usually in the building. They had a lot in common, in that they all shared histories of abuse and neglect, and four of the group were fostered or in care. In the all-girls comprehensive school they were a recognisable group of disaffected, low achieving, low self-esteem girls.

The hopeful feature of this group is that they were attending school – not just to 'have somewhere to go', perhaps, but for more profound reasons. There may have been a hope that something about their experience might be understood. They might have been acting out their sense of being left out, of little value, feelings of hopelessness in the face of learning and a sense of being disregarded and un-noticed whilst finding some solace (and attachment) in the safety of a peer group/secure base. The building and the predictable routine and responses within the institution were perhaps sufficiently containing for the girls to remain in the institution with some sense of hope. It was decided to plan an intervention around their presence rather than to engage in conflict about their disruption.

> In an adolescent day unit, attendance rates were high. The young people were also 'persistent attenders'. The large communal lunches may have been the real attraction! But the same young people frequently attempted to steal from the building. The safe was kept in a locked and steel strengthened cupboard in the middle of the building. The house was frequently broken into, and it was evident that the focus of attention was the safe, despite our letting the young people know that there was little in there. They tried to break into the door, the barred windows and even the brickwork. It was an almost tedious event. It seemed as if they were drawn to the building, and, in particular, to the safe at the heart of the building as if hoping to find something there.

Winnicot (1964) comments that stealing can be a reaching out for something that has been valued in the past, an unconscious longing for something that was good. To our staff group it felt as if the building and the safe were symbols of a hope, a place where the young people might find something good that they unconsciously longed for. But when faced with real opportunities for relating to each other and to the workers, feelings and intimacy were rejected and disparaged. It was as if they were at a very primitive stage of emotional development, able to attach themselves to objects and places but not yet able to value themselves or others.

Brain development and containment through feedback

Schore (2000) points out the use-dependent nature of the brain, and the rapid right brain development in infancy which can become dominated by fight-and-flight pathways leaving little development of the capacity to think. He also recommends therapeutic intervention in which a relationship with a sensitive and attuned other can begin the process which begins or develops the capacity for relatedness and reflectiveness. Understanding the meaning of the communication behind the behaviour becomes a starting point for the experience of being held-in-mind and understood. The point of crisis, when fear is triggered, is a vital time for the teacher to hold onto thinking, to be non-reactive and to communicate some understanding. It is at this point that new pathways can begin to form, which provide alternative ways of responding other than fight-and-flight.

Given the brain's potential for regeneration and growth throughout life, frequent positive feedback can also help to develop and reinforce more positive responses. Wherever possible, positive comments about achievement, whether about behaviour or in terms of the task, help this process.

In the context of school such a position of informed understanding is hard to hold when faced with often severe provocation. The importance of agreed procedures and responses and colleague support cannot be overemphasised, in order to protect the teacher as well as controlling reactivity for the child.

Emotional containment and the network

Adults working with children of such histories usually experience high levels of anxiety themselves, as they experience the nerve-wracking uncertainty of how pupils may react and respond on a daily basis. Unexpected eruptions, aggressive attacks on others, persistent refusal to co-operate or focus on the lesson, disruption and absence of respect and sympathy towards others are wearying experiences on a daily basis and attack the thinking capacity of the teacher. Powerful projections of unprocessed procedural memories can trigger reactions in others which can replicate the original perceived abuse (see Chapter 3, and Chapter 8 – *Behaviour as a source of teacher stress*). It is easy to feel angry and rejecting towards such pupils and in care, they often experience repeated fostering breakdown. The opportunity to restore the capacity to think is essential, or the system becomes reactive and acts out the child's experience of thoughtlessness and abandonment by punitive responses and exclusion.

Reflection can be practiced by regular meetings of the network of professionals associated with the particular pupil. Preferably, such meetings should be regulated by a need for consistent support and review and not by crisis. The network may be within the school; the class teacher, mentor, LSA, SENCo and head teacher can become the reflective and supportive network. Outside agencies; mental health (CAMHS), social services, foster carers can also be included, so that anxieties can be shared, splitting and blaming can be avoided, and consistent and appropriate strategies can be developed which are proactive and not reactive.

The workers benefit from professional and non-critical understanding and support. In particular, the network becomes the emotional container, strong enough to withstand attacks and sustain thinking. Boston & Szur (1983) and Hopkins (2000) write vividly about the power of the rage which such children experience and the effects of this within therapeutic relationships. It is the practice of supportive reflection which prevents punitive and reactive responses to often extreme provocation. This is further discussed from the perspective of the teacher in Chapter 8.

Nature of the task

As has been discussed, the task is a valuable tool in working with pupils who find relationships threatening. For these children in particular it is a stimulus to the left brain function whose protection is needed against right brain reactivity. However, interest in the outside world, investigation and curiosity may have been experienced as dangerous. The nature of the task for these pupils can also be experienced as a humiliating reminder of inadequacy and denigration likely to trigger reactive behaviour. Core experiences related to early adverse experiences may affect distance and spatial awareness, a sense of time and basic numeracy (Beaumont 1999).

The child's learning can be at a primitive stage; acknowledging the developmental stage rather than his or her chronological age is a useful starting point in differentiating tasks. Concrete, mechanical and rhythmic activities which engage left brain function can be soothing to highly charged states. Counting, colouring, sorting, building structures, sequencing objects/pictures, copying, can be starting points. Rhythmical physical exercise and music can have a regulating influence on brain rhythms. A creative intervention in a small group of primary pupils with emotional and behavioural difficulties was to begin the day with cross-stitch, and many teachers now use 'brain gym' to calm and focus pupils at regular times in the day. Finding a metaphor related to symbolic containment, buildings, houses, boats and bridges, and the value of metaphor in stories are also valuable tools. The curriculum is rich with opportunities to explore feelings and situations without reference to self. Engagement with an appropriately do-able and differentiated task is the starting point in finding safety and interest in learning.

Strategies for emergencies

Despite good practice, unpredictable situations occur. Low level anxiety triggers, of which others are unaware, can result in a sudden eruption of violence or distress. Talking at the time of incidents is usually unhelpful when the fight/flight pattern is engaged. Confrontation is likely to escalate the situation. It is helpful to remind oneself at such a time that eruptions of aggressive behaviour are often triggered by fear and when apparently most aggressive, children can actually be at their most afraid. To engage in the confrontation can exaggerate the fear and escalate the incident. Stepping back is a first step. Understanding that fear often fuels aggression can help to begin to change the reactive process in the child.

At such times it is more useful to immediately engage the 'safety routine'. For younger children, this can mean removal to a safe, quiet, unstimulating place, a quiet corner or the room of a senior teacher who is perceived as powerful/safe, and being given a box of concrete routine activities. This was christened by one girl as her 'worry box'. For older pupils, a permission card can be produced to be shown to the teacher, and the pupil can then remove themselves to a 'place of safety' without the need for confrontation. Once reactivity has calmed, the incident can be talked through and the child can return to the classroom. This protects the teacher, other pupils and the child in question from escalation of fear and perceived danger. It requires forward planning and collaboration but can reassure and restore functional capacity.

Derek had been sent to a quiet room to recover from an outburst in Year 4 class. He raged around the room, cursing and swearing at the detention he had been given in response to his behaviour in class. I wondered about how helpless he might feel when he was told what to do by the teacher. He began to jump into the cushions calling out that he was a baby. His behaviour became quite alarming as he became more and more infantile, crying out in a baby voice. I worried about the impact of my comment and how I would restore his proper state in order to return to class. Meanwhile he knocked over an enormous box of felt tip pens. I asked if he would help me to pick them up. I wondered how many there were of each colour. He suddenly seemed interested and began to gather up the pens colour by colour, counting them. By the time all the pens had been found and counted, Derek was very calm and organised, soothed by the careful process of putting them back in the box. He seemed to recover some sense of himself and voluntarily returned to class quite calmly.

Inadvertently I had asked the right question, which enabled a switch to left brain function and the return of self-control. Such questions can be useful tools in enabling reactive behaviour to shift.

△ △ △ △ △ △ △ △

In the head's office, six year old Shelly, extremely challenging, was present as the head and I made plans for a review of Shelly with her class teacher. Shelly had been difficult in class and had been sent to the head for time out. I wondered what tasks Shelly was given to do when she was sent out. The head described how Shelly liked to sit at her desk and pretend to be the headteacher. She had been allowed to practice her own form of self-regulation – omnipotently assuming the role of the adult as she did in the classroom when she dictated to the teacher. Perhaps a small desk with pretend office jobs would have been more appropriate and enabled Shelly to play at being in charge whilst experiencing the safety of the head's room and her authority.

Later, Shelly settled well in a school where the head was very firmly in control and his office was clearly his territory.

△ △ △ △ △ △ △ △

Colin, aged eight, had become much calmer in the classroom. He no longer suddenly attacked the teacher and could sit and focus on work. At a review his teacher reported that the strategies she had implemented had more or less worked and Colin's behaviour had improved. There had been no recent unprovoked outbursts. However, it had been a challenge to her to remain calm, hold to the strategies and respond in an uncritical and non-reactive manner. At the meeting, she described how Colin was loudly tapping on the table with a ruler, and making an irritating disruption in the class. Feeling very irritated and angry herself, she wanted to shout, "STOP TAPPING THAT RULER". Instead, she summoned up her patience and quietly said "Perhaps you can let me have the ruler please Colin", and to her relief, he handed it to her. The teacher was able to respond to Colin's behaviour with a calmness which suggested that she could contain the anxiety which was triggering the disruption.

It is easy to get things wrong in the face of such challenges, and demanding to really insist on getting things right. The language that is non-challenging and led by 'thank you for …' rather than 'please get …' is likely to be less provocative. In the long run, the leading task with such reactive children is to reduce the dominance of the 'fight-and-flight' brain response and to permit other experiences to build a different pattern. Self moderation is then more possible and opens up the opportunities for learning and relationships.

Summary

- This small but significant group of children can readily be identified from infancy and present very challenging demands on teachers and to school resources. Their needs are great, both for practical and early therapeutic support. The implications for the future, if their needs are not adequately met, can be disastrous for themselves and others, as well as highly costly in financial and social terms.

- It is strongly recommended that an assessment of possible Attachment difficulties is included in early assessment of pupils causing concern.

- It is also recommended that a category of 'developmental vulnerability' is introduced, which may help to formalise planning within a professional network which is collaborative, consistent and committed to a long term programme of intervention across the age range. Without this, the crisis and reaction continue, with decisions determined by crisis intervention rather than a response which acknowledges the needs of the child and protects the teacher and others from the incessant anxiety that the child can trigger.

Chapter 8

School as a Secure Base for pupils and teachers
From reaction to reflection

> As John Bowlby never hesitates to mention, 'a society which values its children must cherish their parents' (Steele 2002)
>
> ... and perhaps their teachers too!

In previous chapters, the experience of teaching and learning has been examined using the framework of Attachment Theory to explore aspects of individual pupil behaviour in school. The Attachment model suggests that the core outcomes of secure attachment are:

- a capacity to tolerate frustration and uncertainty
- a sense of self as worthy of affection and respect
- a capacity to relate to others with sensitivity and respect
- a sense of personal agency.

These are clearly aspects of response and behaviour which would support positive engagement in learning and social inclusion.

However, as has been discussed, adverse attachment experiences can affect these capacities, and the pupil/teacher relationship in particular, with implications for behaviour and achievement.

Success in school can be undermined by:

- little capacity to tolerate frustration or uncertainty
- anger with those who are perceived as 'letting you down'
- low self esteem
- insensitivity to the feelings of others
- lack of trust in adults

At a moderate level, these behaviours can be understood and accommodated within the good practices and ongoing relationships of the school community (Rogers 2004). However, at a more extreme level, the behaviour can cause significant distress to others, and, in a cumulative way, can cause considerable and significant distress to teachers whose work is interrupted, whose skills can be disregarded, and who can feel themselves to be, and sadly sometimes are, attacked. For all pupils, understanding the experience behind the behaviour informs and strengthens the effectiveness of the planned intervention.

This chapter seeks to examine the nature of this experience more closely and to propose a practice which aims to reduce teacher stress and develop a more supportive framework for vulnerable pupils. This can be achieved by providing a professional framework in which talking, reflection, thinking and planning are the tools used to explore and resolve complex behavioural issues which challenge classroom practice – the Work Discussion Group. This practice mirrors Bion's Theory of Thinking (1967) and Bowlby's conditions for Secure Attachment, whereby anxiety is transformed into thought by understanding and reflection. Teacher and pupil benefit from the same process.

Behaviour as a source of teacher stress

Most teachers experience satisfaction and interest in their work. It is also true that when faced with the often relentless challenge of difficult pupil behaviour, teachers can become demoralized. Pupil behaviour is at the top of the list of stress factors identified by teachers. This is likely to be expressed as varying levels of disruption, aggression, high noise levels, poor attention span and withdrawal

(Pratt 1978)

Caspari (1976) commented

… exhaustion felt by most teachers at the end of term is more closely linked to the demands made on the skills and personality of the teacher in keeping discipline over the children he teaches than in any other aspect of the work   (p.29)

Recent incidents of extremely challenging pupil behaviour have caused teachers to call for increased powers of exclusion (Observer 19th May 2002). Over the years, the increased burden of accountability through bureaucracy has increased the potential for stress, but there is no doubt that for many teachers the experience which can be most distressing is repeated challenging behaviour.

As discussed in previous chapters, and Chapter 7 in particular, pupils bring their difficulties, frustrations and uncertainties into the learning situation, with particular expectations of how the teacher will respond. The relationship between teacher and pupil is fraught with meaning. It is a relationship which is imbued with attachment significance and affected by unconscious processes. These derive from early experiences described in previous chapters. In the absence of sufficient support at appropriate times, psychological defence mechanisms develop to defend against excessive anxiety – defence mechanisms which prevent a breakdown in emotional function. In the absence of sufficient support on an ongoing basis, the child's behaviour can become organized around an almost constant defensive state. This excludes the possibility of being able to think. Instead, strong feelings which have not been contained by the secure base can be split off and projected – other people can begin to feel the anger, fear or humiliation which is unbearable to the child.

- An example of this is the disregard and disrespect of others. Those who have been humiliated or disregarded themselves can act this out towards others and so relieve themselves briefly by witnessing the other person's – or the other child's humiliation. The pupil who laughs when another gets the answer wrong may have been anxious themselves about 'getting it wrong'. Strongly critical behaviour can be a reflection of feeling highly criticized oneself. In a primary classroom a girl who was living in Local Authority Care persistently attacked another child who had been taken into foster care, as if punishing him for being 'bad'. She was unable, perhaps, to bear her own feelings of being 'bad' and unwanted.
- Another example of this is bullying. The child who frightens others is often very frightened themselves and unable to bear being afraid. The 'victim' is then made to experience this fear and the bully is no longer persecuted by his fears. Behind bullying and aggression may lie a great deal of fear. De Zulueta describes this rapid transition between feelings of fear and rage in her book *From Pain to Violence – the Traumatic Roots of Destructiveness* (1993).
- Pupils who feel humiliated by their own apparent lack of skills can denigrate others for being successful, and paradoxically, adopt the attitude that 'being clever is stupid'. This can be a strong mutual attraction in

disaffected peer groups who then feel even stronger in attacking the others who are perceived as 'clever'.

- Pupils who themselves feel unwanted, left out and 'different', can lead attacks on others who are perceived as having slight but recognisable differences and heap insults upon them, sometimes with devastating consequences.

These projections of unwanted feelings can permeate school cultures and be very destructive.

In many respects, teachers are inadequately prepared for responding to such challenges. There is little training for working with pupils with emotional and behavioural difficulties in initial teacher training. It tends to be the choice of teachers or mentors already involved in the 'specialism'. Support for pupils with emotional and behavioural difficulties tends to be located outside the school, in external support services which hold the 'expertise'. INSET is usually dominated by a focus on the requirements of delivering the curriculum rather than on the experiences of teaching and learning. Also the teaching profession, in which individuals work on a face-to-face basis with the whole range of the population, has no inbuilt mechanism for teacher support or supervision, unlike social work or medical worker colleagues.

In this respect, when teachers and other education staff are overwhelmed by the demands of anxious children, the experience of adverse attachment can be replicated. The teacher can become reactive and respond with rejection, criticism and punishment. The pupil can re-experience the overwhelming uncertainties of early infancy which were not adequately contained in the primary Attachment relationship. Behaviour patterns developed in response to this, such as those described in Chapters 5, 6 and 7, can be triggered and so the cycle of insecurity and insensitivity goes on. In secondary schools in particular the pupil may turn to the peer group as a substitute secure base for acceptance and affirmation; this is not always a positive choice. Drugs and alcohol can provide the dulling effects desired to relieve states of high anxious arousal.

In schools where there is least collaborative thinking about challenge and distress, the most likely it is that strong feelings are being constantly projected into the school community. There can be a sense of uncontained fear running about the school, "as if anything can happen".

What can the teacher do? The Work Discussion Group as the Secure Base for teachers and pupils

Hargreaves (1978) described teachers as 'suffering from progressive exhaustion made worse by lack of supportive relationships amongst colleagues. The problem stemmed from not being able to admit you have a problem because this implies that you are incompetent. Offering to help a colleague implies that they *are* incompetent'.

Two very different responses are possible when teachers seek support.

> *In the very early days of being a teacher I walked into the staff room distressed by my continuing difficulties with Janet in Year 7 science lessons. I approached my friends in the staffroom saying, "I can't manage that girl. She drives me mad and spoils the whole class". My friends nodded sympathetically as another teacher called loudly across the room, "I don't know what you're talking about, I don't have any trouble with her in my class".*
> *I felt humiliated and hopeless at a time when I hoped for support and help.*

Hanko (1995) comments 'Failure to support their staff in responding appropriately to pupils' emotional, behavioural and learning difficulties and in coping with their own feelings and anxieties about difficult-to-teach children is shown as not only increasing such childrens' needs but as hindering all-round effectiveness of teachers and schools' (p.146). When such support is available, the difference in outcome can be significant for the pupil and the teacher.

The example above contrasts sharply with the changes possible when support is forthcoming.

> *A teacher in a special school had become very angry with a boy whom he described as perpetually bad tempered. In the workshop group with other teachers, he described the difficult aspects of the boy's life that may have caused the boy to feel confused and frustrated, helpless and angry. This helped the teacher to distance himself from the projections of anger from the boy, and to think about the boy's feelings. Later, when the boy again came in from the playground in an angry state, complaining that something unfair had happened to him, the teacher remained calm and said to him that he understood how unfair things sometimes felt, how frustrating that must be and how awful that could make you feel. The teacher described the boy as becoming calmer, walking to his seat and able to get on with some work – a rare occurrence. The teacher reflected that he had been able to make the boy feel understood, even though he could not affect the source of his distress, and that this had made a difference*   *(Geddes 1996, p.109).*

The teacher's deepened awareness of the meaning of the pupil's behaviour had led to a better outcome for himself and the pupil. The teacher's anxieties about the child's behaviour had been thought about and 'contained' by the group of colleagues. The teacher could then use his knowledge about the child to begin to understand his experience and so the possible meaning of the boy's behaviour. In turn, the teacher could contain the strong feelings of despair in the child and transform them into an understanding which made a difference. Reactivity provoked by the boy's behaviour no longer interfered with the teacher's capacities to think, and thus he was able to respond more constructively.

In the teachers' Work Discussion Group, and over time, the developing understanding of the meaning of behaviour was reflected in the strategies that were evolved in response to subsequent challenging situations.

The Work Discussion Group as the Secure Base for pupils and teachers

The secure base described in the context of Attachment Theory is the emotional and physical refuge in which uncertainties are processed into thoughts and the base from which exploration can take place. Transformed into a process to help teachers in the school setting, the joint Work Discussion Group meets these criteria.

This model of working was developed by Caplan (1970) and adapted to the educational setting by Gerda Hanko. Her pioneering work is described in her book *Special Needs in Ordinary Classrooms – from staff support to staff development* (1985, 1990, 1995). In it are described the setting up, procedures and practice of The Joint Problem Solving Workshop, upon which the work discussion group is modelled. This well-tried model of teacher consultation, supervision and support is based on creating a safe space in which teachers and others working with children in schools can present their experiences of challenging pupils or groups. With the support of colleagues, they can deepen their understanding of the issues and meaning of the experience and seek appropriate and achievable strategies of intervention to bring about a better outcome for the pupil, class and teacher. Reaction is transformed by reflection into the capacity to plan and make an appropriate response.

The process and procedure

The process of the work is important and models much of the secure Attachment characteristics based on trust, sensitivity and containment of anxiety.

- The regularity and predictability of the time and meeting place mean that the teacher knows that there is support available; anxiety about a situation is more easily contained until the group meets again.

- The membership is a regular and committed group who develop a trust in each other's support and respect, uncontaminated by rivalry or criticism. Hanko describes how the language of communication helps to facilitate trust and mutual support.

- Confidentiality is agreed so that disclosure about work and pupils is contained and respected.

- Members are invited to present a situation which they are finding difficult or challenging concerning a pupil or a class. It is essentially pupil/work focused. The presentation is as detailed and honest as the teacher is able to be so that all aspects of the experience can be considered.

- Information concerning the pupils' history is very useful, and helps the group to make sense of confusing behaviour.

- The sharing of challenges and successes becomes a forum for professional development whereby the whole staff group becomes more informed and skilled in a wide range of situations.

- The structure of the group is important and allows time to;
  - present the problem
  - permit questions from the group to clarify the situation
  - reflect upon meaning and
  - formulate intervention founded in a deeper understanding of the difficulty.

- Holding consistent boundaries of place and time ensures that the whole process is fully experienced and maintains a sense of safety. A usual session may be one and a quarter hours.

• The presence of a facilitator from outside the school is an invaluable presence who can hold the time boundaries, maintain an overview, support the group when sensitive issues are being discussed as well as contribute a different perspective.

As a result of collaboration, thoughtfulness about pupils and shared contributions about interventions, teacher groups become more able to integrate emotional and cognitive experience for pupils causing concern. Teachers and other colleagues working with the identified pupil develop a shared understanding of the pupil's experience and a sense of the meaning and communication implicit in their behaviour. This can be transformed into a consistent and agreed intervention plan throughout the school. The thoughtful work discussion group incorporating all staff, becomes the *secure thinking base* within the school, primarily for the teacher. But ultimately it will strengthen the containing qualities of the school for the pupil. Such a thinking group is also able to bring together an understanding of the pupil's emotional and cognitive experience and help in the pupil's psychological integration. It is a highly recommended practice which is not only a form of professional development but a significant contribution to improved whole school practice. It was also noted that in an evaluation of a series of groups in primary school (Geddes 1991), fewer referrals were made to outside agencies, reflecting an increased capacity to support and include a wider range of pupils in the school. This practice reverberates with inclusion policies.

An example of a group discussion demonstrates this practice, and also reflects issues which affect many schools.

Cooper & Upton (1991) encourage us to pay attention to the context in which pupil and teacher experience their various demands and stresses. Rutter (1975) pointed out that 'behavioural difficulties and low attainment in reading are much commoner in schools with high rates of teacher and pupil turnover. Schools which lack stability of staffing and which had a high proportion of children coming and going were those with the most problems.' (p.202)

In just such a situation, an experienced teacher talked about her experiences with her class.

The class in question was a newly constituted Year 4 class. For several months they had been taught by a succession of supply teachers who had all left after only a few weeks. The room was described as being in a shabby, run-down state with tables spread around the room and the resource cupboards and screens in the middle, breaking up the space into unconnected areas. There was pupil work on the walls but it was hard to see amidst the muddle.

The teacher complained that the pupils were constantly noisy and they did not listen to her. They wandered and ran about the room and were unsupportive and critical of each other. They were very messy and did not want to clear up. Most important, the teacher reported that she felt like a poor teacher, unwanted by her class. The teacher aired her anger, resentment and humiliation.

After some time it seemed possible to think about how the children were feeling. The group wondered about what the shabbiness and mess might indicate about the pupils' feelings. The teacher thought about their possible feelings of being 'rubbished' by repeated rejections by a succession of supply teachers. She related this to her own feelings of being ignored and rejected by the class. We talked about the class not listening to anything she said and how this made her feel as if she was useless and unimportant. She wondered how the class must feel because they did not have a teacher of their own. She thought about the tables organized into separate islands and wondered about the lack of cohesion as a class. She realised that it was hard to recognise the pupils' good efforts because of the mess that they made.

The more these issues were thought about the more the teacher felt that she had 'taken on' the feelings of the pupils. Her sense of being useless and unwanted and unliked were perhaps how they felt and not how she had felt before beginning work with the class. An example of the power of 'projection'. This awareness enabled her to step out of the projected feelings, regain her own self esteem and professionalism and develop strategies to tackle the problems of the class.

Strategies for reorganizing the classroom, displaying work and instigating different clearing up procedures resulted in sufficient change in class behaviour to enable the teacher to assert her position with the class. The teacher subsequently reported working with colleagues on new themes and projects for the next term. The teacher and the class had begun to function again and some weeks later she reported feeling proud of her class and of their achievements. She had also decided to stay on at the school.

In these ways, unconscious inter-personal processes of reactions, projections and defences can permeate relationships and systems, affecting pupils and teachers alike. In a profession in which relationships are a core aspect of the work, such experiences are inevitable. However, projections 'felt' by the teacher can be a form of communication, which can help him or her to understand the pupil's difficulties; in the above example, these were explored by the group, and this helped to expand understanding of the pupils' feelings.

In the current political context overall educational concern and directives are driven by measures of performance and achievement, published as lists which identify schools as achieving or failing. The teacher can experience a conflict between concerns about performance and concerns about pastoral care. Little time may be spent on reflecting about how pupils may feel. It is worrying to note that often this is expressed in schools as a division of responsibility; between learning and welfare – between cognition and emotion – between practice and process. Teachers can be focused on curriculum and performance and the pastoral needs of pupils can be the concern of mentors and support staff. This represents the possibility of a significant split in schools' capacities to think about pupils causing concern unless there is a managed policy to bring both aspects of the pupil experience together by discussion and shared thinking. These kinds of potential divisions of thinking can be bridged in the collaborative framework of the Work Discussion Group which represents the whole staff group.

It is also my experience that as the process becomes more skilful and more collaborative over time, it becomes the forum in which the most severe behavioural challenges (such as those discussed in Chapter 7) can be contained. Together, staff can agree upon and develop the consistent strategies and interventions which are most likely to make a difference to the 'disorganised' pupil, and protect the teacher and others from the potentially deskilling and demoralizing experience of relentless challenging behaviour. Exclusion may not be the only option.

Characteristics of 'School as a Secure Base'

Schools can 'make a difference' and do have the potential to be emotionally and mentally healthy institutions when the match between educational goals and pupil developmental and emotional needs can coincide. Attachment Theory helps us to construct a school as a 'secure base' in which pupils can function effectively both emotionally and cognitively. The basic requirement of the practice and ethos of the school would thus reflect the needs of staff and pupils and are common features of most good practice.

For pupils this would reflect:
- respect for all pupils no matter what their skills and difficulties
- a building which is safe and adequately supervised
- sensitivity to the meaning of communications implied by behaviour – empathy
- predictable, reliable routines
- a fast response to absence – noticing the absent pupil
- consistent rules and expectations framed around keeping pupils, staff and the building safe
- familiar long term relationships – pupil feels 'known'
- modeling of good relationships between adults
- informed reflection about incidents rather than reactivity
- a system of disciplinary procedures which is fair to all – and non-abusive.

For staff this would reflect:
- strong leadership which listens to all staff and who can be relied upon for consistent, available support – a professional container
- respect for the physical comfort of staff – the well-kept staff room as a symbolic secure base!
- a capacity to reflect on difficulties when they arise, rather than react in an   unthinking way

- mutual support and collaboration across the whole staff group
- a common language and framework for understanding pupils' behaviour
- a regular forum for review of difficulties in a reliable and supportive group.

Within such a framework, the school can become a surrogate 'secure base' which can contain the inevitable anxiety engendered by the challenges of learning. Additionally, the school will be providing compensatory relationships and experiences to pupils, whose capacities to learn have been impaired by adverse emotional and social experience.

Early intervention and prevention

However, in order to really make a difference to the behaviour issue, prevention is clearly the desirable option. Many initiatives and projects exist to meet the needs of underachieving children who are often identified by challenging behaviour. Some of these are long term statutory agencies with enormous experience and familiarity with local schools. Other such as the BEST teams target deprived and needy areas. There are other initiatives such as the Youth Inclusion Team, Youth Offending Teams, local Youth Workers and often other supportive agencies working closely with local schools and communities. In my experience, all are excellent workers doing valuable work. It is however, a reactive service depending on the child causing someone some concern, and is also often led by the challenging behaviour of acting-out boys. Sure Start marks the beginning of a different process, that of early identification and intervention within the community with vulnerable infants and carers. This intervention could be carried on into education within the existing framework of schools and support services.

A proposed prevention/intervention pathway within the primary education framework

In the small, more intimate community of primary schools, individual difficulties can be easily noticed and prioritized. There is more possibility for intervention at the inter-personal level and for integration of early intervention programmes into the policy and practices of the school.

In the Early Years, vulnerable pupils can be readily identified. The capacities to engage in play, communicate with others and relate appropriately to adults and to peers are key areas to observe and assess; they fore-shadow the relationships highlighted by the learning triangle of pupil, teacher and task presented in Chapter 4.

For pupils causing some concern and for whom there is no identifiable learning difficulty, then an emotional developmental assessment may be appropriate. Such tools are available. The Boxall Profile (Benathon & Boxall 1998) was developed for this purpose. It is a carefully structured and evaluated assessment, a Diagnostic Developmental Programme used to:

*   assess pupil need
*   plan intervention
*   and measure progress.

The Boxall Profile has been used in conjunction with Nurture Groups (Nurture Group Network) in primary and secondary schools. Children identified and assessed by this process are taught in small groups – the Nurture Group, where their individual needs and developmental delays are addressed. The content is not led by the curriculum but by the identified needs of the children. The Nurture Group aims to develop the skills and resilience necessary to access the curriculum, and has been evaluated and found to be extremely effective in bringing about long term change for very vulnerable pupils.

By identifying areas of developmental need both at an emotional and experiential level, and combining this with understanding the Attachment and social issues which can affect behaviour and learning, primary schools can incorporate highly effective intervention practices with powerful implications for individual development for all pupils.

It is then possible to see a continuum of identification and intervention strategies for vulnerable children stretching:

- from Sure Start and other community based programmes which support children and families,
- through Nurture Group intervention in early primary school,
- supported by individual therapeutic interventions such as those of educational therapists (Caspari Foundation), whereby social and emotional blocks to learning can be addressed through individual or small group work
- via transition preparation
- and into secondary schools

Focus on early identification and effective intervention is likely to maximise pupil emotional well-being and resilience so essential for entry into secondary school, where the challenges of a big and diverse institution make greater demands on the pupil's capacities to face uncertainty and engage in learning.

Conclusions

- Schools can and do make a very significant contribution to emotional well being of children and families with implications for achievement, social inclusion and mental health. Education is also the clearest route to achievement and inclusion in later life, especially when the skills and capabilities of all pupils are respected.

- Such a contribution is likely to be made when all staff share a common language for understanding and responding to the meaning of pupil behaviour. The links between pupil experience in school and experiences of early relationships is clearly made here and elsewhere.

This book strongly recommends...

- That Attachment Theory, and the outcome of associated research, is adopted as a relevant framework for understanding and responding to pupils' difficulties and should be a core aspect of teacher training and professional support and development.

- That teachers and others seek to respond to the meaning of behaviour rather than react to difficult feelings.

- That schools adopt a policy of talking and reflecting in a facilitated and structured setting, as both a means of strengthening the school's capacity to contain anxiety for staff and pupils, and of enhancing learning and achievement for all pupils – to turn reaction into reflective intervention.

- That an integrated early identification and intervention system be embedded in primary education, aimed at maximizing support for vulnerable pupils and minimising the characteristics of early experience which can interfere with emotional development, learning and social inclusion.

The education setting is probably the greatest opportunity we have, outside the family, to promote and maintain childrens' social well-being. This is most likely to come about when emotional well-being becomes built into the education agenda and into the structure of educational practice. Insights derived from Attachment

Theory and research help in this process, and can make a significant contribution to developing an ethos of emotional well-being in schools, to strengthening the possibility of future inclusion, and to reducing the likelihood of disaffection and anti-social behaviour as today's young children become tomorrow's adults in the wider world.

Bibliography

Ainsworth, M.D. (1967) *Infancy in Uganda: Infant Care and the Growth of Love* Baltimore: John Hopkins Press

Ainsworth, M.D.S. & Wittig B.A. (1969) Attachment and exploratory behaviour of one-year-olds in strange situation, in B.M. Foss (Ed) *Determinants of Infant Behaviour,* Vol.4 London: Methuen

Ainsworth, M.D.S., Blehar, M., Waters, E. & Wall, S. (1978) *Patterns of Attachment – a Psychological Study of the Strange Situation.* Hillsdale N.J.: Erlbaum

Ainsworth, M.D.S. (1982) Attachment – retrospect and prospect in C.M.Parkes & J. Stevenson-Hinde (Eds) *The Place of Attachment in Human Behaviour.* London: Routledge

Arende, R., Gove, F., & Sroufe, A. (1979) Continuity of individual adaptation from infancy to kindergarten: A predictive study of ego-resiliency and curiosity in pre-schoolers. *Child Development,* 50, 950-959

Arnold, E. (1977) *Out of Sight – Not Out of Mind* British Association of Social Workers Publications, Birmingham p.26-35

Atkinson, J. (1989) Developing a whole-school approach to disruptive pupils in R. Evans (Ed) *Special Educational Needs – Policy and Practice* Oxford: Blackwell Education

Balint, M. (1959) *Thrills and Regression,* London: Hogarth Press

Barnet, L. & Bain, A. (1980) *The Design of a Day Care System in a Nursery Setting for Children Under Five* Occasional Paper 8, Tavistock Institute of Human Relations: London

Barrett, M. & Trevitt, J. (1991) *Attachment Behaviour and the Schoolchild,* London: Routledge

Barrett, M. & Varma, V. (Eds) (1996) *Educational Therapy in Clinic and Classroom* London: Whurr

Barrows, K. (1984) A child's difficulties in using his gifts and imagination in *Journal of Child Psychotherapy,* V.10

Beaumont, M. (1988) The effect of loss on learning in *Journal of Educational Therapy* Vol.2, 1: 33

Beaumont, M. (1991) Reading between the lines in *Journal of Psychoanalytic Psychotherapy,* Vol. 5 No. 3, 261-269

Beaumont, M. (1999) Children, learning and the meaning of time in *Journal of Educational Therapy and Therapeutic teaching* Issue 8

Benathon, M. & Boxall, M. (1998) *The Boxall Profile – Handbook for Teachers* from The Nurture Group Network, 307, Spitfire Studios, 63-71, Collier St, London N1 9BE

Benathon, M. (1992) The care and education of troubled children in *Therapeutic Care and Education* 10,1, p.37-49

Bentovim, A. (1992) *Trauma Organised Systems. Physical and Sexual Abuse in Families* London: Karnac

Bion, W. (1967) A Theory of Thinking in *Second Thoughts: Selected papers on Psychoanalysis* London: Karnac

Blance, E. & Cook, A. (1990) *Monster* series, Longman

Boston, M. & Szur, R. (1983) *Psychotherapy with Severely Deprived Children* Routledge Kegan Paul

Bowlby, J. (1944) Forty Four Juvenile Thieves – their character and home life in *International Journal of Psychoanalysis,* 25 p.1-57

Bowlby, J. Maternal Care and Mental Health (1951) *World Health Organisation Monograph* Series 2

Bowlby, J. (1953) *Child Care and the Growth of Love* London: Penguin

Bowlby, J. (1969) *Attachment and Loss. vol. 1, Attachment* London: Penguin

Bowlby, J. (1973) *Attachment and Loss. vol.2 Separation: Anxiety and Anger* London: Hogarth Press

Bowlby, J. (1980) *Attachment and Loss. vol.3 Loss: Sadness and Depression* London: Hogarth Press

Bowlby, J. (1979) *The Making and Breaking of Affectional Bonds* London: Tavistock Publications

Bowlby, J. (1988) *A Secure Base* London: Routledge

Bretherton, I. & Waters, E. (1985) Growing Points of Attachment Theory and Research *Monographs of the Society for Research in Child development* 50 (1-2, Serial No.209), U.S.A.: University of Chicago Press

Briggs, R. (1975) *Father Christmas goes on Holiday* London: Puffin

Britton, Feldman & O'Shaughnessy (1989) *The Oedipus Complex Today* London: Karnac

Caplan, G. (1970) *The Theory and Practice of Mental Health Consultation* USA: Basic Books

Caspari, I. (1976) *Troublesome Children in Class* London: Routledge Kegan Paul

Cohen, A. & Cohen, L. (1986) *Special Needs in the Ordinary School – a source book for teachers* London: P.C.P. Education Series

Cooper, P. & Upton, G. (1991) Controlling the urge to control: an ecosystemic approach to problem behaviour in schools in *Support for Learning* vol.6 no.1 p.22-26

Coopersmith, S. (1967) *The Antecedents of Self-esteem* San Francisco and London: Freeman and Co.

Davou, B. (2003) Unconscious processes influencing learning in *Journal of Psychodynamic Practice* Vol.8

de Zulueta, F. (1993) *From Pain to Violence: The Traumatic Roots of Destructiveness* London: Whurr.

DfES (2001) *Promoting Mental Health with Early Years and School Settings*

DfES (2003) *Every Child Matters*

DfES (2004) *Promoting Emotional Health and Wellbeing*

Dowling, E. & Osborne, E. (1985) *The Family and the School: A Joint Systems Approach to Problems with Children* London: Routledge and Kegan Paul

Emanuel, R. (2000) *Ideas in Psychoanalysis: Anxiety* UK: Icon Books

Engeland, B. (1983) Comments on Kopp, Krakow and Vaughn's Chapter in Perlmutter, M. (Ed) *Minnesota Symposium in Child Psychology* Vol. 16 pp.129-135, Hillsdale, New Jersey: Erlbaum

Erickson, M.F., Farber, E.A., Engeland, B. (1982) Antecedents and concomitants of compliance in high-risk pre-school children. *Paper presented at the annual meeting of the American Psychological Association*, Washington D.C.

Erickson, M.F., Sroufe, L.A. & Engeland, B. (1985) The relationship between quality of attachment and behaviour problems in pre-school in a high-risk sample in Bretherton and Waters (Eds) Growing Points of Attachment Theory and Research (1985) *Monograph of the Society for Research in Child Development* 1985, 50, 1-2

Fairbairn, W.R.D. (2003) *Psychoanalytic Studies of the Personality* London: Brunner-Routledge

Fonagy, P., Steele, M., Steele, H., Leigh, T., Kennedy, R., Mattoon, G. & Target, M. (1993) Attachment, the reflective self, and borderline states in S. Goldberg, R. Muir & J. Kerr (Eds) *Attachment Theory. Social, Developmental and Clinical Perspectives* Hillsdale, New Jersey: Analytic Press

Fonagy, P. (2001) Psychoanalysis and Attachment Theory. London: Karnac

Freud, A. (1989) Normality and Pathology in Childhood. London: Karnac

Galloway, D., Ball T., Blomfield D. & Sayd, R. (1982) *Schools and Disruptive Pupils* London: Longman

Garner, P. (1993) Exclusions: The challenge to schools *Support for Learning* Vol.8 No.3

Geddes, H. (1996) Educational therapy and the classroom teacher in Barrett, M. & Varma, V. (Eds) *Educational Therapy in Clinic and Classroom* London: Whurr

Geddes, H. (1991) *An examination and evaluation of the role of two teacher support groups in developing more effective educational practice with pupils with emotional and behavioural difficulties in mainstream classrooms* MA dissertation at Roehampton Institute of Higher Education

Geddes, H. (1999) *Attachment and Learning: an Investigation into links between Maternal Attachment Experience, Reported Life Events, Behaviour Causing Concern at Referral and Difficulties in Learning* PhD Thesis, Roehampton Institute at University of Surrey

Geddes, H. (1999) Attachment, Behaviour and Learning – implications for the teacher, the pupil and the task in *Journal of Educational Therapy and Therapeutic Teaching* Issue 8

Gerhardt, S. (2004) *Why Love Matters – How Affection Shapes a Baby's Brain* London: Brunner-Routledge

Grossman, K.E. & Grossman, K. (1991) Attachment quality as an organiser of emotional and behavioural responses in a longitudinal perspective in Parkes C.M., Stevenson-Hinde J. & Marris P. (Eds) *Attachment Across the Life Cycle* London: Routledge

Hanko, G. (1985, 1990, 1995) *Special Needs in Ordinary Classrooms. From staff support to staff development* Oxford: Blackwell

Harlow, D.H. Love in infant monkeys (1959) and Harlow, H.F. & Harlow M.K. Social deprivation in monkeys (1962) in *The Nature and Nurture of Behaviour Readings from Scientific American* (1972) Open University

Hargreaves, D.H. (1975) *Interpersonal Relations and Education* London: Routledge Kegan Paul

Hargreaves, D.H. (1978) What teaching does to teachers *New Society* 43, 9.3.78

Hargreaves, D.H. (1984) *Improving Secondary Schools: Research Studies* London: ILEA

Holmes, J. (1993) *John Bowlby and Attachment Theory* London: Routledge

Holmes, J. (2001) *The Search for the Secure Base. Attachment Theory and Psychotherapy* London: Brunner-Routledge

Hopkins, J. (1987) Failure of the holding relationship: some effects of physical rejection on the child's attachment and on his inner experience *Journal of Child Psychotherapy* Vol.13 no.1

Hopkins, J. (1990) The observed infant of attachment in *Journal of the Institute for Self Analysis* Vol 4 no.1

Hopkins, J. (1996) From baby games to let's pretend in *Journal of British Association of Psychotherapists* 31 p.20-28

Hughes, D.A. (1997) *Facilitating Developmental Attachment. The Road to Emotional Recovery and Behavioural Change in Foster and Adopted Children* Jason Aronson Inc Northvale: New Jersey

Johnson, L. (1992) Educational applications of attachment theory in *The Irish Journal of Psychology*, 1992, 13, 2, 176-183

Jordan, J. (1974) *The Organisation of Perspectives in Teacher/Pupil Relations : An Interactionist Approach* unpublished M.Ed Thesis, University of Manchester

Kalu, D. (2003) Containers and containment *Journal of Psychodynamic Practice* Vol.8

Karen, R. (1998) *Becoming Attached. First Relationships and How They Shape Our Capacity to Love* Oxford: OUP

Klein, M. (1952) Some theoretical conclusions regarding the emotional life of the infant and our adult world and its roots in infancy (1959) in *Envy and Gratitude and other Works* 1946 to 1963 London: Hogarth Press

Kolvin, I., Garside, R.F., Nicol, A.R., Macmillan, A., Wolstenholme, F., Leitch, I.M. (1981) *Help Starts Here. The Maladjusted Child in the Ordinary School* London: Tavistock

Laslett R. (1977) *Educating Maladjusted Children* London: Granada Publishing

Lubbe, T. (1986) Some disturbed pupil's perceptions of their teacher: a psychotherapist's viewpoint *Journal of the Association of Workers for Maladjusted Children* Vol. 4 no.1

Main, M. & Cassidy, J. (1988) Categories of response to reunion with the parent at age 6: predictable from infant attachment classification and stable over a one month period *Developmental Biology* 24: 415-26

Main, M. & Solomon, J. (1982) Discovery of an insecure-disorganised/disorientated attachment pattern in Parkes, C. M. & Stevenson-Hinde, J. (Eds) *The Place of Attachment in Human Behaviour* London: Routledge

Main, M. & Weston, D. (1982) Avoidance of the attachment figure in infancy: descriptions and interpretations in Parkes C.M. & Stevenson-Hinde J. (Eds) *The Place of Attachment in Human Behaviour* London: Routledge

Main, M., Kaplan, N. & Cassidy, J. (1985) Security in infancy, and adulthood: a move to the level of representation in Bretherton, I. & Waters, E (Eds) Growing Points of Attachment Theory and Research (1985) *Monographs of the Society for Research in Child Development* Vol.50 nos.1-2

Maslow, A.H. (1954) *Motivation and Personality* New York: Harper

Mongon, D. & Hart, S. (1989) *Special Needs in Ordinary Schools – Improving Classroom Behaviour: New Directions for Teachers and Pupils* London: Cassell Educational

Moore, M-S. (1998) How can we remember but be unable to recall? The complex function of multi-modular memory in Sinason, V. (Ed) *Memory in Dispute* London: Karnac Books

Morton, G. (2000) Working with Stories in Groups in Barwick, N. (Ed) *Clinical Counselling in Schools* Routledge

Parsons, C. (1994) Excluding primary school children in *Family and Parenthood Policy and Practice* London: Family Policy Studies Centre

Perry, B.D. (1994) Neurobiological sequelae of childhood trauma: PTSD in Children in Murberg, M. (Ed) *Catecholamines in Post-Traumatic Stress Disorder: Emerging Concepts* Washington D.C.: American Psychiatric Press

Pratt, J. (1978) Perceived stress among teachers: The effects of age and background of children taught *Educational Review* 30, 3-14

Robertson, J. (1952) Film: *A two year old goes to hospital* London: Tavistock Child Development Research Unit.

Robins, L.M., West, P.A. & Herjanic, B.L. (1975) Arrests and delinquency in two generations of black urban families and their children *Journal of Child Psychology and Psychiatry* 16: 125-140

Rogers, B. (2004) *How to Manage Children's Challenging Behaviour* London: Paul Chapman

Rutter, M. (1975) *Helping Troubled Children* London: Pelican

Rutter, M., Maughan, B., Mortimore, P., Ouston, J. (1979) *15,000 Hours* Somerset: Open Books

Saltzberger-Wittenberg, I., Henry, G. & Osborne, E. (1983) *The Emotional Experience of Learning and Teaching* London: Routledge Kegan Paul Ltd

Schermbrucker, R. & Daly, N. (1989) *Charlie's House* South Africa: David Philip

Schore, A. (1994) *Affect Regulation and the Origin of the Self* Hilsdale, NJ: Lawrence Erlbaum Associates

Schore, A.N. (2000) The effects of early relational trauma on right brain development, affect regulation and infant mental health in *Infant Mental Health Journal* Vol.22, 201-269

Sendak, M. (1967) *Where the Wild Things Are* London: Bodley Head

Shepherd, M., Oppenhein, B. & Mitchell, S. (1971) *Childhood Behaviour and Mental Health* London: University of London Press

Sinason, V. (1992) The effects of sexual abuse on intelligence in *Journal of Educational Therapy and Theraputic Teaching* (1992) Vol.1 no.1

Sinason, V. (1995) Lecture *What is the Sense in Stupidity* Taunton Association for Psychodynamics, Spring Conference 1995

Sroufe, L.A. (1983) Infant-caregiver attachment patterns of adaptation in pre-school: the roots of maladaptation and competence in Permutter M. (Ed) *Minnesota Symposium of Child Psychology* Vol.16 pp.41-81

Sroufe, A. (1986) Appraisal: Bowlby's contribution to psychoanalytic theory and developmental psychology; attachment: separation: loss *Journal of Child Psychology and Psychiatry* Vol.27, No.6, pp.841-849 1986

Steele, H. (2002) State of the art: attachment theory in *The Psychologist* Vol. 15 no. 10

Steig, W. (1979) *Amos and Boris* New York: Scholastic

Stern, D.N. (1985) *The Interpersonal World of the Infant* London: Basic Books

Stern, D.N. (1977) Missteps in the dance in Boon (Ed) *The First Relationship* Boston: Harvard University Press

Suess, G.D., Grossman, K. & Sroufe, L.A. (1992) Effects of infant attachment, mother and father on quality of adaptation in pre-school: From dyad to individual organisation of self in *International Journal of Behavioural Development* 15, 433-65

Underwood Report (1955) *Maladjusted Children* London: HMSO

Varley, S. (1984) *Badger's Parting Gift* Collins

Verschueren, K. & Marcoen, A. (1999) Representation of self and socioemotional competence in kindergartners: differential and combined effects of attachment to mother and to father in *Child Development* 70, 183-201

Waters, E., Wippman, J. & Sroufe, L.A. (1979) Attachment, positive affect, and competence in the peer group: two studies in construct vaildation in *Child Development* 50, 821-829

Waters, T. (2003) The therapeutic use of story writing in *Journal of Psychodynamic Practice* Vol.8

Wellington, B. & Austen, P. (1996) Orientations to Reflective Practice *Educational Research* Vol. 38 No.3

Williams, L.M., O'Callaghan J. & Cowie H. (1994) Therapeutic issues in educational psychology: can attachment theory inform practice? *Educational and Child Psychology* Vol.12 no.4 p.95

Winnicott, D.W. (1955) *Playing and Reality* London: Pelican

Winnicott, D.W. (1964) *The Child, the Family and the Outside World* London: Pelican

Winnicott, D.W. (1965) *The Maturational Process and the Facilitating Environment* London: Hogarth Press

Winnicott, D.W. (1971) *Therapeutic Consultation in Child Psychiatry* London: Hogarth Press

USEFUL CONTACTS

Caspari Foundation for Educational Therapy and Therapeutic Teaching 1, Noel Rd, London N1 8HQ
www.caspari.org.uk

Separation and Reunion Forum, 54-56, Pheonix Rd, London NW1 1ES www.serefo.org.uk

The Nurture Group Network 307, Spitfire Studios, 63-71, Collier St, London N1 9BE

Index